Stand Tough

B Neil Brown

Flashover Press

FLASHOVER PRESS

This Flashover Press paperback edition February 2014

ISBN: 978-1311632340 (ebook)
ISBN: 978-0615982182 (paperback)

DEDICATION

To my son:
Having the opportunity to watch you grow into the honorable young
man you are has made all of this worth it. I love you kiddo.

To my father:
I am the man I am because you are the father you are. I wouldn't be
this strong if you hadn't made me this way. Thanks Dad.

For my mother:
For all the coffee, and all the love you brought with it!

CONTENTS

PART ONE

INTRODUCTION

September 28th, 2010. I was admitted into the emergency room of Regional Medical Center in Madisonville. It was my second trip into that ER within a week's time, and it was nearly my last trip anywhere. Soon after my admittance, my body ceased to function. I was revived and was rushed to Intensive Care, where I would spend the next three weeks barely clinging to life. I only know this because I have been told the story by my family, my friends, and my doctors. You see, I don't remember any of it.

Not. A. Thing.

I can remember things from about a week before that fateful September night, but to understand me - and my story - we are going to have to go back much further into my memory, and my past.

I grew up in a small town in a rural county in Western Kentucky. My father is a Viet Nam veteran, a retired underground coal mine mechanic, and a hair stylist. (Yeah, that's right. My old man fought for our country on foreign soil, dug coal for twenty years, and can still roll a mean perm set!) My mother has been a hair stylist for as long as I can remember, and has owned her own salon since I was eight years old. When my father retired from the coal mines, he went to beauty college so he could work with mom at the salon, and he still does to this day. I played football and wrestled in grade school and high school, fought with both my brothers as all siblings will do, and generally made my parents as miserable as any high school kid can. At home and at school I did my best to do what I was told, stay out of trouble, and be a good son. When I wasn't at home or at school I was a rabble rouser, a fighter. Stubborn as a mule. Why do you need to hear about this now, you might ask? Because what made me that way then would be one of the reasons for who I would grow to be in my life later, and will explain much about how I have dealt with the things that have been thrown at me in life.

1-OUT IN THE WORLD

When I graduated high school I tried college for a bit. But I enjoyed parties and those of the female persuasion too much to be bothered with a formal education. I moved out of my little small town and relocated to a slightly larger small town right down the road. I ended up being room-mates with one of my best friends, at least until he up and got married. Of course, I wasn't too far away from that, and by the tender age of twenty I was married myself. By the age of twenty-two I had a full time career, a wife, and a bouncing baby boy. Of all the things I have done in my life, that little boy will always be my best and most perfect accomplishment.

My career at the time was in the pest control industry - and it put food on our table and a roof over our heads for many years. It wasn't the thing in my life I was passionate about, but it was something I was good enough at to make money.

I was perhaps twenty-five when I found the thing I truly loved to do, which was fighting fires. By this time, my wife and I had divorced. I only got to see my son on the weekends, and I wanted something to do that put a bit of spark into my life. My younger brother Wes had recently joined our hometown fire department, and being as I had just moved back to town, I thought I might give it a try. That was the worst - and best - decision I ever made in my life, joining that department. I have lost a lot of sleep over the years for the phone ringing or a pager going off calling me into the station, but I wouldn't have had it any other way.

Providence Fire/EMS was the place I truly learned what teamwork was all about, and what it really meant to trust someone with your life. I learned what it was to work until you were so weary you couldn't go on, and then go on anyway. As a volunteer, you always start out doing the worst of the "gopher" work. If something needed to be cleaned, you cleaned it. If hose needed to be rolled, you rolled it. Air bottle low? Well, let me show you how to run the air-machine so you can fill those up!

I never minded doing that work, because all I really wanted to do was help out. And I did every chance I got. I did the grunt work for so long that one day I hardly noticed that when I looked up I was actually fighting fires. Looking back now on those very early days at the department, I realize we all did the same grunt work. It just didn't seem nearly as fun when you didn't get to play with the attack lines. We all rolled hose, we all filled tanks, we all did the dirty work. That's what fire fighters do, and that is what teamwork is. It just seems much more rewarding and less like plain hard work when you do it with an air pack on and a hose in your hand.

It didn't take very long for me to become a semi-permanent fixture around the place. Dispatch called and I was there. City siren sounded off and I was there. Gas leaks, car fires, structure fires, automotive accidents with injuries. Brush fires, now those were something I truly disliked. Why, you might ask? You put them out with - essentially - a snow shovel with a blade made out of rubber. They are called "flappers," and I will let you ponder how a fire rushing through ground cover is put out with one of those. No fun. Ever.

I can't remember the first ambulance run I went on, but I can remember going out to assist with patient transfers and transports when the EMT's needed an extra hand. I never enjoyed ambulance runs as much as working a fire, but when they needed the help I went and helped. The department really needed an extra hand with the ambulance runs, so they asked me to go to EMT First Responder school. Of course I told them I would. My first responder school was an accelerated course, and there were only two of us in the class. Instead of three hours a night two days a week, it was eight hours a night five days a week.

Keep in mind that I was only a volunteer, and I was working ten hours a day at my full time job in the pest control industry. So midnight fire runs, first responder class, and all the other things at the department, were done in the evenings after I got home from work. I didn't mind though, because I was doing something I really enjoyed.

Less than two years after I began volunteering at the department, I was offered a real -paid even - part time job at our station. Back then, our department worked four-man paid crews per shift. Everyone had to be able to make ambulance runs as well as fire runs. If we had a fire at the same time we had an ambulance run, that meant we had two fire fighters on the fire ground and two off somewhere in the ambulance. When that happened, off-duty fire fighters were called in along with the volunteers. Two fire fighters are simply not enough to tackle a fully engulfed structure.

So, not only were the full time guys working twenty-four hour shifts every other day, they would get called in for ambulance runs and fires on their days off. These guys were hardly ever home, and on working weekends they would be away from their families for seventy-two hours straight. A part-time fire fighter could fill the gap and give the guys some much needed breathing room.

One evening, I was fighting a fire only about six houses down from mine, on the same street. We all worked very hard to keep it contained and keep the house off the ground. I spent most of my time on the roof with an axe and a pike-pole looking for hot spots and cutting ventilation holes. I remember that roof and that night well, because when I came down off that ladder and the fire had been put out, our assistant chief Brad Curry asked me to come sit down and talk to him on the tail-board of the fire engine.

Honestly, I thought I was in trouble. Volunteers don't always get to go play on the roof, and I thought I had gotten caught with my hand in the cookie jar. You could have knocked me over with a feather when Brad asked me if I wanted a paid part-time position. I was surprised to say the least. I never thought of myself as good enough to be a paid man. Now I will confess to the fact that I am only an average fire fighter. I simply always showed up when they needed help. I took the job, and that decision, along with what I learned from my many years of service to the community, would shape who I am in this life and how I would deal with adversity.

2- REAL LIFE

By the time I had taken the part-time position at the fire department that little boy of mine was out of diapers and had begun kindergarten. I had gotten remarried, bought a house, and received a promotion at my job with the pest control company. The extra income from the department was nice, but it certainly put pressure on my family life.

With my new marriage came two beautiful little step-daughters, so I had to try and juggle a wife, shifts at the department, kids, soccer coaching, the house, and the career. And that pest control job had become a career. My promotion landed me a position that kept me away from home several nights a month, and an office three hours away in Louisville, KY.

I might be in the far western reaches of the Purchase Area of Kentucky in the morning, and get a phone call telling me I was needed in the rolling hills of south central Kentucky in the afternoon. My job entailed driving wherever we had an account with a possible problem, and fixing it. Several years before my company had gotten into trouble with the state agency that oversees chemical application, and my sole purpose was to find the mistakes someone else made and fix them. Honestly, thirteen out of my seventeen years with the company was devoted to fixing other people's mistakes. I spent a lot of time on the byways of the bluegrass State killing termites and irritating branch office managers. When I wasn't on the road I was back home trying to have a life and a family, and work at the fire department, too.

During one particularly rough patch when the fire department was under-staffed, a typical week for me would consist of waking up out of my bunk at the station on a Monday, putting on my pest control uniform, and leaving for my day job. I would work all day on the road, come home to see my family for an hour or so, then put the fire department uniform back on and go back to the station to take an over-night shift. I would get out of the station bunk the next morning to repeat the process for the rest of the week. If I had to work at the station on a weekend I would clock in at 7:00PM on a Friday evening and then clock out at 7:00AM the following Monday morning.

There were weeks that I wouldn't sleep in my own bed at home, and if I wanted to see the kids my wife had to bring them to the station to visit. As you could imagine, this got old, but it needed to be done. I grew up watching my father go to work on swing shifts at an underground coal mine job he disliked, but he did it regardless because he had a family to support. I was doing nothing more than what my father would have done, and I had the luxury of at least enjoying the work that I did.

Working nights at the station wasn't always a bad thing. The pranks everyone played and the jokes everyone told kept it from being monotonous, and if we didn't get any calls, we could sleep through the night on the clock. More often than not, though, the 911 phone would ring and the dispatcher would send us out. Late evening and early morning calls weren't bad, but those middle of the night ambulance and fire runs always ruined your sleep.

Eventually the department got back up to full staff and my eighty hour "part-time" work settled down to something a bit more reasonable. I was finally able to enjoy the home I had bought, hang out with my son and step-daughters, and sleep in my own bed beside my wife. I got to make my son's tee-ball games, and coach my step-daughter's soccer games.

I have to say that having little girls in the house was quite a change for me. They were sweet-hearts and cutie-pies, but they were nothing like having a boy in the house. If all you have are girls, or all you have are boys, you will never truly understand how conniving little girls can be and how brutally honest boys can be with their fathers. Essentially, I think girls are too smart for their own good and boys are way too dumb. When something got broken in the house or someone did something they weren't supposed to do, the children's reactions to questioning were polar opposites. Little girls are smart enough to lie, and little boys are dumb enough to tell the truth. The girls would lie and blame whatever had happened on someone else, all the while batting their eyelashes at and acting like sweet little angels. On rare occasions they might even tear up a bit, if they thought it might help their situation. The boy, on the other hand would always tell the truth.

Little girls seem to know when they have done something wrong, and little boys don't. It is just in the nature of kids. Of course, this can work to your advantage. Always get the story out of the boy first, just a helpful little parenting tip to all you new parents out there. I will never complain about my son being honest with me. I have always tried to teach him that the truth will always get him in less trouble than a lie will, and even now at his late age of nearly eighteen, he will be honest with me about some of the silly stunts he has pulled.

I used to laugh at my mother when I would tell her about things I had done or stunts I had pulled that she wasn't aware of, and she would say, "I could have lived the rest of my life not knowing my son did something that like that!"

Sorry, Mom. I now totally understand where you were coming from with that.

Children's antics aside, I was really settling into my life as career man, husband, father, and part-time fire fighter. I was following in the footsteps of my dad, taking care of my family, and really beginning to enjoy life. I should have known something was going to go wrong.

3- I HAVE WHAT?

One morning, somewhere around the turn of my twenty-eighth birthday, I woke up to a sore mouth. Not really the whole thing, just right under my tongue. I got up, had my coffee, had my shower, and got dressed for work. It has become a habit of mine over the years that the very last thing I do before I leave the house is brush my teeth. When I brush I always like to give my tongue and the surrounding areas a through scrubbing, as well. When you see six or seven different clients a day having less than foul breath can be rather important.

My sore lower palette had been pushed to the back of my mind until I dove into some halitosis destroying tongue scrubbing. I suddenly felt like I had a wasp loose in my mouth and it was none too happy about the accommodations! After a careful rinse and spit, I studied the soft tissue on the floor of my mouth below the tongue. To my surprise I found three tiny, round, white spots that were very tender and painful to the touch. I decided I might need to see a doctor, so I asked my wife to call and make me an appointment at the clinic and I went to work.

The next few days that lead up to my appointment were not really that bad, I just had to watch how I chewed my food and the spots were not a problem. When I finally got in to see the doctor, she decided I had canker sores, and asked if I had changed any of my eating habits recently. *Well there you go*, I thought. That was simple. I explained to the doctor that I had recently found my favorite citrus flavored soda pop in a diet flavor, and I had been drinking quite a few. She told me all I needed to do was go back to the regular as opposed to diet and all would be well again. I trotted out of the office with a prescription in hand for a canker sore gel to use and got back to life. I stopped drinking the diet soda, used the prescription, and all was well again. That is, until I got a spider bite.

Working around the underside of houses puts one in rather close proximity to all sorts of creepy crawly things, and it was only a matter of time until I got bitten by something. That something, according to doctors, was a brown recluse spider. If you have never seen one of these spider bites, they can be gruesome, and there was one right on the front of my left shin. Work even paid for the doctor's office visit because they assumed the bite happened on the job. The bite got a bit nasty, but then cleared up with treatment, leaving me a small rounded scar.

Again, all healed, all better until I found another bite on the same leg, and a day later another behind the bend of my knee. I called shenanigans on the whole "spider bite theory" and went to see a different doctor. It was a good thing I did because my mouth had begun hurting again, and I seemed to be getting - of all things - a case of hemorrhoids.

So let me roll that up for you to ponder again: Three so-called spider bites, canker sores in my mouth, and -- that's right -- hemorrhoids. Let me tell all you young gentlemen out there that may or may not ever experience pain in that general area, you don't want it, much less having to broach that subject with your father to ask his advice. I had a hemorrhoids talk... with my father. He gave me good advice on what to do to relieve that pain, but it didn't help me. And I still had to tell my old man that it hurt to go number two at the age of twenty-eight. Where was WebMD when I needed it?

I finally made it into a new doctor's office to get another opinion. The kids were with my mom, and the wife was with me. A doctor was going to be looking at my hind-end; she had better be there to hold my hand. I had my pre-doctor nurses' interrogation, where I got to explain all my problems to her, and then she left looking rather bewildered. When the doctor made his entrance I was ready for the worst, but was pleasantly surprised to meet a fresh-faced young doctor doing his residency. I don't know why that made me feel better, but it did. He proceeded to have a look around in my mouth at the nearly nickel sized canker sores, looked at the supposed bites on my legs, and then had the presence of mind to not act embarrassed when he told me he needed to look at the hemorrhoids.

Have you ever seen a sigmoid scope? No? Do you remember those little scopes the doctors would use to look into your ears when you were a kid? Well, when I saw the thing that is the first thing that came to mind. Old Dr. Hall, pediatrician for many years in my hometown, would pull his little ear scope out, tug on my earlobe, jam the scope in my ear, and make little bird tweet noises. He would tell me he saw birds in my ears, and then tell my mother that everything looked fine.

"Tweet tweet" had somehow burbled up from the

hellish depths of my memory when I saw this scope that looked like it had been scaled up to fit in an elephant's ear, and he was going to put that where? Yeah, he was gonna, but then he didn't. Why? Because he saw right away that I didn't have the dreaded piles, I had something much worse. I had canker sores in all the soft exterior tissue down there.

Hindsight being what it is I would have preferred it had been 'roids.

It was a very lucky thing that this was the doctor I saw that evening. Being a resident, he still devoured the medical journals at every opportunity, and just that afternoon he had read about a very rare disease that happened to fit all my symptoms. Skin lesions on my lower extremities, aphthous ulcers in my mouth, and aphthous ulcers at the exit of my lower GI tract. He called it Behcet's Disease, and I cried like a baby on the way home from the doctor's office that night.

4- ALWAYS FIGHTING

I used to have a saying that there were only two things that scared me in life - my God and my father. As long as what I was facing didn't involve those two, I would fight-fight-fight for what I wanted or how I wanted things to go. As I write this I am forty years old and I still can't stand up to my old man. He still can make me shake in my boots after all these years. God no longer has that effect on me, but that is a different subject, entirely.

Why do I tell you this? Because one of the things that makes me stubborn - makes me a fighter - is the fact that if I couldn't stand up to my father, than I was going to stand up to everything else and anyone else in my life.

Growing up in school or a home I did everything I could do not to raise the ire of my dad. One of the scariest sounds I can remember from my childhood was a leather belt clearing belt-loops. That meant me or one of my brothers had screwed up, and an ass-whipping was in order.

So, you can imagine how much I didn't do things wrong where my parents could find out. I remember once getting into a fight in the high school gym locker room. The guy I got into it with slugged me a few good times and I didn't even fight back, just sort of kept the worst of the punches from landing. When it was all said and done, no one ever found out. I didn't tell a teacher, I didn't tell the principal, I just sucked it up and went about my business.

I didn't know how the old man would react to me getting into a fight and getting suspended, so I kept my mouth shut. That is just how I did things at home and at school. Lay low, get decent grades, do decent at sports (that my parents wouldn't even come watch anyway) and stay out of trouble. Let me clarify that last. Dad was generally working or sleeping during game times, and mom worked a lot, also. I know they made some of our football games, but no one ever went to one of my wrestling meets. Years later my mother would tell me that she was too afraid to see me get hurt. They didn't ignore our sports; they simply couldn't always make it.

So, when I wasn't at home or at school I made it a point to not back down from fights and foolishness. When I got my license and my first car I spent as much time out of county as possible. Most of my friends lived in other places, and that was where I went. Also, there was less chance for word of my antics getting back home so I went a bit wild. Standing on the mall parking lot in Madisonville, KY, I learned to be stubborn, to stand up to anyone that thought they were better than me, and to put anyone on the ground that wanted to ball up their fists or puff out their chest. I didn't win every fight I got into, but I won enough that I got left alone, or if it looked like I was going to involve myself, that other people backed down. What does all that have to do with Behcet's, or losing my limbs?

Everything.

That is one of the reasons I am who I am. That

fight and streak of stubborn-ness that made me stand up to anything and everything, trying to prove to myself that even if I couldn't stand up to my old man, I could still be a man. That there are only two things in the world I was afraid of, and if you weren't one of those two things, I would go down fighting to prove that you couldn't beat me.

That attitude is what kept me going at the age of twenty-eight when I was diagnosed with BD. I wouldn't let it beat me, I couldn't. During the worst of those times I still got up every day and went to work. I still went on fire runs and ambulance runs and came in every time the fire department needed me. The fire department was probably the best thing for me, at the time. Working at the station taught me more humility than I had ever had in my life, and taught me it isn't always about being the best, but about always trying and not giving up.

So I didn't give up.

Not long after my diagnosis I got another promotion at work. It meant a little more money, a lot more territory, and a lot more responsibility. I had no other option but to take the job, knowing that it would either make or break my career. All the while that I transitioned into my new position I was still dealing with all the BD problems. Sometimes I would go days without talking because my mouth hurt too much, or was too full of ulcers.

I would go for weeks at a time without eating solid food because BD had saw fit to put ulcers in my throat. I couldn't swallow. Being constantly hungry and constantly in pain makes a guy pretty grumpy, let me tell you. Add in the ulcers that kept popping up on my body in strange places and you could imagine how much constant misery I was in.

But I still got up and worked, still did my best to be a dad and a husband, and still went in when the station called. That was all I could do. I was put through every test imaginable by the doctors. Behcet's Disease, you see, is so rare that if doctors get a chance to play with a BD patient they won't turn it down. I couldn't tell you how many times I went to the doctor for a normal everyday illness to have some specialist push their way in with my regular doctor because they wanted a glimpse of the "Behcet's Patient."

I was once admitted to the emergency room for pneumonia while I happened to have a large BD ulcer on my leg. Before my doctor had an opportunity to start treatment for the respiratory infection, another out-ranking doctor burst into the room demanding for me to strip down because she wanted to see the wound on my leg. I told her no, and she grabbed my leg and proceeded to pull up my pant leg so she could look anyway.

She got a stout cussing from me, and didn't get to see the ulcer on my leg. This was a normal occurrence, and most of my doctor's visits ended up like that. I would go in for one thing, and get tests or exams for something else, all to satisfy the curiosity of the doctors who had never poked or prodded a real live BD survivor. And that's what I was, a survivor. Most patients diagnosed with BD don't survive very long. Those that do can plan on having a miserable life.

I finally stopped dealing with most local doctors when an oncologist who happened to be treating me at the time decided I needed to have bone marrow drawn from my hip to be studied. If you have never had this procedure, I would not recommend it unless it is medically necessary. Essentially the doctor will take a hollow drill bit and hammer it into your hip until it reaches bone marrow depth, then pull out a plug core of your bone and marrow to run tests on. That test was done more than ten years ago and I still feel the spot when I stand just right.

I assumed the test would ultimately do me some good, but to my chagrin I found the test wasn't for my benefit. It was done to satisfy the curiosity of my doctor. I had been through a six thousand dollar procedure to satisfy an arrogant doctor's curiosity. I had to pay that bill. I did. Then I walked out of the Mahr Cancer Center and never looked back.

We ended up trying all kinds of things to treat my disease, but nothing really seemed to work for long. Experimental medications would work for a bit then the BD would come back full force. All the normal medications I was given just seemed to make me more miserable, so I couldn't take those for very long. I became involved with online message boards with other BD sufferers and we traded stories and treatments, along with words of encouragement.

During those times on the forums I found people time and time again asking me how I did what I did. I had all the same symptoms as everyone else, but I still held a job and took care of my family. I couldn't understand what they were asking. They thought I had some hidden secret or some special medicine I simply wasn't telling them about that made me able to keep up with life, as well as the sore joints, constant pain, and inability to eat.

All I could tell them then was that I had responsibilities to attend to and I would just grit my teeth and go about my business. Believe it or not this made me somewhat of a celebrity among those early internet Behcet's sufferers. I hadn't given up when everyone else had. I can remember a BD newsletter that used to go out via email to the subscribers to those boards, and I was the subject of a story in it. There was a picture of me in my turn-out gear as well as one of me in a rescue harness hanging off the side of the building.

That story and those pictures generated more correspondence than I knew how to deal with, and they all read the same. "What's your secret?" and "You really inspire me" was the common theme. I couldn't understand what the big deal was. All I was doing was the same things I had always done, fighting to keep going and making myself stronger than the pain. I just didn't give up when I could have, I kept on going. I have found throughout all my ordeals that this hasn't changed, and the response that I get always stays the same. I would get asked, "How do you do it?" and I would respond, "How do I not?"

I lived that life for two more years, and at the age of thirty my life began to implode.

5- KEEP ON KEEPING ON

Those first two years dealing with my Behcet's Disease were by far the roughest. I was constantly working, constantly sick, and constantly miserable. On top of the BD, I had many challenges at work, a legal case involving my son, and a wife that was growing more dissatisfied with her life. She hadn't signed on to be the wife of a grumpy sick guy.

I was mostly relieved when she told me she wanted a divorce, but the timing was not so great. I was going to school at night to upgrade my EMT license, work was blowing up during the day, and we had just sunk quite a few dollars into the custody battle. My stress levels were at an all-time high, and while this was not what I needed, it was what I got. So I dealt with it.

Stress is a trigger for BD, and the stress from that period in my life brought on one of the worst bouts I have ever had with the disease. I remember standing near the kitchen sink at my parents' house telling them about my impending divorce, and having to scratch the outside of my right calf because it itched. I didn't think much about it at the time, but that little itch would be at the top of my mind for the next several years.

In the midst of my second divorce my company

decided they needed me far, far away in the city of Lexington, Kentucky, all day, every day. I really didn't want to move, so I spent the better part of a year living out of a hotel room off of I-75. Getting away from home was, in reality, the best thing that could have happened to me, and Lexington has got to be one of my favorite cities to work in.

All of the back roads in and around Fayette County are lined with wonderful stone fences, and you can't throw a rock without hitting a horse farm. It truly is beautiful country up that way, and I highly recommend taking a vacation there if you live anywhere close. Downtown you have the campus of the University of Kentucky, and Rupp Arena is a very cool place. I made it a point to plan my days as often as possible to put me downtown at the end of my workday. It was in Lexington where I first learned the pure joy of ordering a large espresso with cream in a Starbuck's and being able to sit down in a big, puffy couch and let the workday stress drain away.

I spent a lot of time in that little coffee shop before I made friends in the area. I still think that downtown Lexington Starbuck's is the best of the chain, and I have been to hundreds of the stores over the years.

I had gotten into mountain bike trail riding not long before the assignment in Lexington, and I very quickly found that the trail systems kept up by the city were top notch.

It was on those trails that I first met what would turn out to be one of my best friends, who would stand with me through many of my life's trials. If you don't have a riding partner on a trail, there are plenty of forums out there to meet up with people and ride, and I met my "brotha from anotha motha" Matthew Williams, on a Kentucky mountain biking forum. I have never been a small guy, and Matthew is stout as an ox and built much the same. We hit it off as soon as we met, and the two of us have ridden literally hundreds of miles of trails together.

I hadn't yet finished my EMT-B school, so when I wasn't working or riding trails I was driving back home every other night to go to class. My class was held in Princeton, and I was working in and around Lexington. Just about every other night for three months I would finish my work day, then drive four hours back for a four hour class, then drive four hours back to Lexington. You might wonder why anyone would want to put themselves through something like that, but I was still fully committed to helping my community and working at the fire department when I could.

Sometimes in life we over-extend ourselves, and our only options are to either cave under the pressure, or buckle down and suffer through until you get it done. The latter has always been the way I try to do things, and that get-it-done attitude has served me well.

So there I was in Lexington, five days a week, home two, working and riding and making runs at the station when I could, and that little itch on my leg had turned into a monster. It had started out as a small aphthous ulcer on my calf, followed not long after by another one a few inches below the first. All you can do for BD ulcers until they heal is care for the wound and apply pressure bandages, so that is what I did. At one time I had around fifty scars on my body from all the BD ulcers that have come and gone. That amount is less now that I am minus a few body parts, and it is now almost a relief that the worst scar I've ever had from BD was taken with my legs.

Those two little ulcers on my calf would grow larger, start to heal, and then start to grow again. I can remember a time very early on where both of them had gotten to be about the size of a silver dollar and then both healed to the size of a mosquito bite, but that was not to last. I was about thirty-one years old when those on my right leg really got going, and I would end up changing bandages on my leg for the next three years.

My worst fear was that the ulcers would get big enough that they grew into one, and I had been warned by doctors if that happened it might grow large enough to require surgery and skin grafts. That is not something I wanted to go through, but what we want and what we get are not always the same. The day I woke up to find the border of the smaller - and lower - ulcer had grown into the larger one above was a horrible day, indeed.

I had very recently found myself given somewhat of a sideways promotion at work, and had found myself working for a new boss. That particular boss was one of my few saving graces at the time. Damon Bayens had risen to the head of my quality control office at work, and I had been lucky enough to work for the man once before when I first started with the company. Damon had been my service manager way back when my son was born, and he actually came to the hospital the night my kiddo came into the world.

Damon knew I was a hard worker, and if I needed to go to the doctor about my Behcet's, he didn't complain, he just let me go. He has a work ethic out of this world, and I learned a lot of my best - and worst - work habits from this former Marine Corps MP. I didn't get to stay long working for the ol' jarhead because he would find himself promoted to branch management, and I would find myself promoted to a regional office.

My job duties didn't really change all that much, but the responsibility and geographic territory seemed to have increased exponentially. Working for the regional office meant having an office in Indianapolis, Indiana, but not ever really having to be there. My range of offices had expanded to include most of Indiana, part of Ohio, all of Kentucky, and a smattering of Illinois, Tennessee, and Missouri. I had to say goodbye to the weekly trail rides with my buddy Matthew in Lexington, but I had not yet said goodbye to the ever growing ulcer on my leg.

The doctors now had a new name for it; Pyoderma Gangranosum. And that big, ugly name fit the big, ugly wound on my leg. It had grown to the diameter of a soda-pop can and showed no signs of slowing or stopping. By this time the mouth and GI tract ulcers had begun to slow down, so at least I went into my new office and new territory without the embarrassment of speaking with a pain induced lisp, or worse: being totally unable to speak. That ended up being a very good thing, as one of the more rewarding periods of my career were about to begin.

I had spent so much time fixing other peoples' mistakes and re-training employees that the company decided I needed to start training and educating all the new-hire employees. On top of all the other things the company had me doing, now once a month I would take a week to travel to Indianapolis (and occasionally Cincinnati, Ohio) to help teach a week long, eight hour a day school to all new employees.

Subjects ranged from termite and pest control to proper paperwork, to not killing yourself with either equipment or chemicals. I really enjoyed this part of my job more than any other, as I didn't have to crawl under any buildings and I could actually wear business casual clothes as opposed to a pest control uniform. I'd like to think I also helped a lot of new employees find their way around the job and the company, but you know what they say about leading a horse to water...

I was still doing my thing at the station on weekends. I wasn't able to work there during the week because I was out of town. But I still did everything I could while at home on the weekends. Every other weekend I had my son, and although I am sure he doesn't remember it like this, he spent a lot of time with my mom and dad so I could make those fire and ambulance runs.

No matter where I might be living in a hotel and working during the week, I always made sure I was back home by 6:00PM on my Fridays so I could pick up my son. Sometimes the time we got to spend on the weekends wasn't much more than dinner out where he wanted and then the short ride to his Grandmother and Granddaddy's house to be dropped off so I could work a shift at the department. I would apologize to him, but I think he understands dear old dad was just doing what had to be done to pay the bills and make a living.

One weekend while working a shift at the station we had a very large structure fire. It seems we had been out on the fire ground forever getting it under control, and the fire boots and bunker pants I was wearing had taken their toll on the BD wound on my leg. The boot was just the right height that with every step the top edge dug into my leg, and I was hobbling around horribly. We had an ambulance run come in, and I think Bradley sent me on the ambulance to simply give my leg a break. I was looking pretty bad, and I didn't have a chance to change out of my fire gear before we got to the patient, so I had to suffer through, anyway. But I did, because the patient and my run partner needed me to.

That, more than anything else, made me decide to start looking farther out and abroad for a better treatment for the Behcet's and my leg. During the time that the wound had been on my leg I had trained in high-angle rope rescue, water rescue, wilderness SAR, as well as urban tactics and had joined (and then become the assistant chief of) the Webster County EMA Search and Rescue Squad. My friend, mentor, and fellow rescue rappel junkie Lee Jenkins had dragged me into more volunteer SAR organizations at the time than I care to think about, and it seemed like all my home time, before and after my second divorce, was spent training or on search operations. I even had the opportunity and honor of training the KY Corrections Department CERT teams in high angle rappelling. Those teams were essentially the prison system SWAT teams, and let me tell you something - there is nothing funnier in the world than a three hundred pound prison guard squealing like a little girl as they break over a sixty foot high wall for the first time on a rope. It is priceless, truly.

I have been on a lot of departments and squads

over my long career in fire/rescue services, and at one time I was active on at least four squads or departments at once. I worked through forty hours straight during the Providence, KY tornado of 2002. I was in the middle of a BD mouth outbreak, and couldn't eat or drink, but I still went in and put my gear on. I couldn't even drive to the station because there was so much debris down on the roads. I walked from my home to my parents' house to make sure they were ok. There I found Lee, and we walked in to the station. We got on our gear, got on the rescue truck, and headed out to clear roads and paths to get to victims and patients.

I dug through the blown over home of a young woman who couldn't find her daughter. I was literally walking over the destroyed walls, sheetrock, and roofing of her little girl's room, sifting through bed clothes and baby dolls hoping and praying if I were to find the child she would be all right. I don't think I have ever been more frantic on the job as I was in that moment, and the relief and joy I felt when the little girl's grandmother came running up with the child thrown across her hip was simply indescribable. The little one had snuck out and run up the road to her Me-Ma's right before the tornado had hit, and she had been asleep in Me-Ma's arms, safe and sound, when the twister came through. Three generations of women stood in the street crying while I picked my chainsaw back up and headed down the way to cut up a tree so a fire engine could come through.

Forty hours without sleep, just going and going and going. The closest thing I got to a nap was standing up leaned against the exterior brick of the station with my gear on and my eyes closed. There were a few of us like that, and I am told that my fellows and I were caught on camera and our stand up nap was broadcast on CNN. During the early morning hours after the tornado I pushed through the BD pain to work triage on countless victims and patients as they were brought in from all over the area. Bandages, splints, cold packs, blankets, and hugs were given out under the cold glare of the generator-powered lights of the fire truck bay.

I made ambulance runs, dodging downed power lines and trees to get patients to the hospital, and then I would hurry back with my partner to wash, rinse, and repeat. To my knowledge, we didn't have a single loss of life from the initial tornado. We had tons and tons of mutual aid from departments within the county and out of the county, and we all worked our asses off to help the people of our devastated little community. I didn't think about my BD pain then, not once.

Through all of that and everything else I had done the Behcet's had never been an issue. Sure, I had hurt a bit, but it didn't get in the way of the job - but this wound that had persisted on my leg was getting in the way and making me a less than effective fire fighter. I wasn't going to have that and something had to be done.

It is amazing how much the internet had grown in the few short years since it had become commonplace. I started -- and ended -- my search for a solution to the (literally) growing problem I had on my leg. There simply wasn't much out there to help BD sufferers specifically. The best clinic in the world at the time was in Japan, and they were still using things like gout medication and steroids such as prednisone. None of the common treatments had worked for me in the past, so I started thinking outside the box.

Behcet's Disease is, at heart, an auto-immune disorder. Many times over the years I have been asked what it is I suffer from, but there are so few BD patients that it is hard for them to imagine. My patent answer has served me well to both put BD into context and describe how bad it can be.

Imagine that all the major and well known auto-immune diseases such as Crohn's, Lupus, Rheumatoid Arthritis, and Inflammatory Bowel Disease all lived in a quiet little neighborhood in a cute little cottage with a white picket fence. They all sit around the kitchen table in the morning enjoying their breakfast and having coffee. When they are done breaking their fast they begin a daily debate as to which one of them has to go down into the cellar where they keep poor Behcet's locked away, chained to the wall, and throw him a raw piece of meat to eat.

That is Behcet's. BD is the bastard child of the auto-immune world. It has practically all the symptoms of all the other auto-immune disorders, and not nearly as many treatment options. At one time or another I have felt the stomach pains of IBS and Crohn's sufferers. I have felt the joint pain and lethargy of Lupus and RA along with the other BD specific symptoms. I was told not long after my diagnosis that I could very well go blind or I might start to get ulcers in the lining of my brain or spinal cord - which would either turn me into a vegetable or leave me paralyzed. This is BD, and this is my world, but I was not going to go down without a fight.

Since I share so many symptoms with other

disorders I decided to start looking at possible treatments for those disorders. I sifted through more government studies and corporate health studies than I can remember, but I wasn't finding anything that seemed like it would help. I nearly gave up my search before I found an obscure mention of a new chemotherapy drug being used with limited success in treating the swollen GI tracts of Crohn's patients. I had to wait six months before research into this new drug was complete and low and behold it became approved for use with Crohn's sufferers.

My only problem was that I didn't have Crohn's, and with a cost of nearly seven thousand dollars for a round of only four infusions, my heart sank. I didn't give up, though, I just changed tactics. I tracked down my original diagnosing doctor and made an appointment in his new office. When I finally got in to see him I was armed with printout after printout on this drug called Remicade, and I did my best to convince my doctor that this was my only opportunity to heal this now softball sized wound on my leg.

I told him of all my trials and tribulations with the specialist doctors he had sent me to, and how they had run test after test without ever helping me get better. If you think I was trying to guilt him a bit you are quite correct, and guilt or not that doctor read all my documentation I had brought him and agreed that he thought it might help. My major stumbling block was that medical insurance would not pay for the treatment for me, because I did not have Crohn's disease. That, I found out, was easily remedied.

It seems since I had all the classic symptoms of Crohn's, so going ahead and diagnosing me with it wasn't a hard thing to do. Plenty of people have had mis-diagnoses over less, and this was going to help me, so it went into my permanent medical records. The only problem I had now was that my doctor, being a general practitioner, was afraid insurance would still turn me down on paying for the chemo if he wrote the prescription, so he asked me to make an appointment with one more specialist, a dermatologist.

As much as I hated going through a specialist again, I did it because my GP told me he would explain everything to the dermatologist so I wouldn't have to. So the appointment was made and I once again submitted myself to a doctor who had seen everything in the world *except* for a Behcet's patient. That trip to the derma's office will always be one of my most humiliating experiences I have ever had while under a doctor's care.

The office visit started out routinely enough, with a nurse doing her pre-doctor thing, and I then sat down to wait for the dermatologist to make an appearance. He did, and rather promptly, as well. It took only a cursory glance at the huge wound on my calf and a look at a few of my more prominent BD scars to make him realize I was the real deal. He was stunned, but also rather pleased that he had a BD patient in his very own private practice! So, what does he do? He decides to treat me like a guinea pig as opposed to a human being. The first thing I had to do if I wanted to get the Remicade script from him was to completely disrobe and allow his nurse to document *every single BD scar I had* with a camera. That was humiliation at its very best. No stone was left unturned, so to speak, and believe me when I say I have some scars in very embarrassing places on my body. It didn't matter though, because this is what had to be done to get the chemo I wanted.

After the awkward photo session was done and I was allowed to put my clothes on and then waited in silence for the specialist to reappear. He eventually did, and he was very excited about all the pictures as well as being involved with the treatment. His plans were to document the treatment progress, and I assume possibly publish something about it. This really put me off, but again, I was more than willing if it would get me my meds and get that wound healed. So we talked a bit more, and he informed me that he would be sending in a nurse shortly with Remicade prescription in hand. I was overjoyed! I was so close to possibly getting rid of this wound on my leg that was old enough to have had a birthday!

When she came in, that little green piece of paper in her hand looked like my salvation, and I could have cried I was so happy. Of course, this is me, and nothing ever seems to work that easily for me. Before she ever handed over the script, she told me the doctor wanted to have me go through a few tests. This was an immediate red flag and I nearly went ballistic. The tests were all about documenting the Behcet's, and had nothing to do with treatment, so I refused. I had told that dermatologist up front that I would not agree to any unnecessary tests, and his answer was to wave that script in front of my nose like a carrot.

I am quite certain his entire staff heard me as I stomped into his private office and told him to go to hell, and informed him that I would sue if any of the pictures he had taken of me were ever published. I walked out of his office without my prescription and with dwindling hope. I didn't even stop at the front desk to pay my co-payment. He sent me bills for that fifteen dollars for years, but I never paid him. I haven't gotten a bill from him in a long time. I guess the asshole finally gave up.

Down but not out, I returned to my GP and told him what had happened - and he agreed that the specialist had overstepped his bounds. With that in mind, my general practitioner sat down and wrote out my prescription for Remicade. We hoped that my medical insurance would accept that expensive of a prescription from a plain old family doctor.

It took six weeks of jumping through hoops, but insurance finally paid up and I had my chemotherapy. Now, along with traveling and teaching for work, taking shifts at the fire department, working rescue squads, and being a father, I could add chemotherapy for three hours a day once a week for six weeks to the list of things I had to do.

6- CHEMO

I had graduated from EMT-B school by the time I started on the Remicade, and that was a really good thing. I couldn't have handled much more on my plate with the way I felt after those once-a-week treatments. I handled them as I always seemed to- I just took the punishment and the pain and kept on doing my thing. Call it stubbornness, but being hard-headed about things like this had always gotten me through before, so I tried it this time as well.

As luck would have it I had changed bosses at work. I still held the same regional office position, but the person in charge of my gig had changed. He was a technical specialist and bug-geek extraordinaire named Tony Bohnert. Tony's main goal with the company was to keep us above board with licenses, certifications, and training. It was Tony who I often ended up teaching new employee schools with, so working with him was never a problem. Working for him was a lot like working with him. As long as I did my job and didn't screw up, Tony was happy.

I was concerned about having to take the time off for chemo infusions, and I had been told trying to drive or work directly after a treatment was a no-no. Tony took it all in stride and never once griped at me for the missed time on those days. Several years later Tony would be diagnosed with colon cancer, and have to go through chemo treatments himself. My chemo was nothing compared to his, and I am glad to report the last time I spoke to Tony he was cancer-free. Tony was a big advocate for this upstart QA guy who was always upsetting people, and he will always be a friend to me. I worried more than anyone within the company might ever imagine when he was diagnosed, and I was always glad to answer the phone when he called - for either work issues or to talk about the pains of sitting through chemo.

Again, Remicade is not nearly as bad as cancer patients' chemo, but it was still no fun, and I made the best of it I could. Because my only option near my home to get the infusions was at the Mahr Cancer Center in Madisonville, I chose to go out of town for my treatments. I still had an extremely bad taste in my mouth over the hip extraction that was unnecessarily done to me there, so I went to the little hospital in Greenville, Kentucky, close to my GP's office.

All I ever dealt with at that hospital were nurses, and they were all great. Of course they were curious about my disease and wounds, as well as the treatment I was getting there. I really don't like putting myself on display, but I also know that seeing the things that Behcet's can do to a body can help health care staff have a better understanding for other patients. My treatments started at 11:00AM and lasted until around 2:30PM every Tuesday. Putting me there right about lunch time, as it were. Because I couldn't stand the thought of eating after the infusion was over, I worked out a free hospital lunch every time I was there in exchange for pokes and prods of my wound by the nurses.

I also ended up getting a lot of free bandages out

of the deal, as it became well known that the BD patient would share his knowledge of his disease, for a price! I was at that little hospital once a week for six weeks straight, and I will tell anyone who ever asks that Muhlenburg Community Hospital has an awesome nursing staff. They made my time there much more bearable.

The treatments themselves were not all that bad. I had a slow drip IV in my arm for three hours, and after the initial sticking, all I had to do was sit and watch the IV bag drip-drip-drip. The afterwards wasn't nearly so fun. I was dizzy, had an upset stomach, and generally felt like total poo until the morning after. I spent many a night at one friend or the other's house puking my guts out and trying not to fall over from the vertigo. The treatments may have made me feel bad, but it only took about the first three infusions for me to see that the growing wound on my leg had slowed its progress.

It had gotten so deep that, uncovered, I could actually *see my calf muscles* bunching and relaxing as I flexed them, and at times I could see some of the tiny blood vessels that wove in and around that muscle. Growth had slowed, but not yet stopped. That took several more months of the Remicade working in my system. My research and internet digging had paid off, and all that I had went through to obtain that treatment seemed to finally be paying off.

Auto-immune disorders are varied in presentation and symptoms, but at their roots they're all the same. If you have an auto-immune disease, you have an immune system that is in some way attacking your own body. Your immune system is always hyped up, and its constantly looking for a fight. Things as simple as a paper cut can be misinterpreted by the immune system as a threat, and your body will kill all the cells around the cut to get rid of it. That is why I had so many BD ulcers and wounds on my skin, every little thing set my immune system off. Bite my lip? BD made sure that tiny little nick became an ulcer the size of a silver dollar. That is how it worked.

The Remicade pretty much killed my immune system. Long after the infusions had stopped I still had to be hyper aware of being around sick people. My immune system was so depleted a simple cold could have put me down. It didn't matter to me, though. No matter what it took, I was not going to let BD or the wound on my calf beat me. So I suffered through with long term in mind. With my immune system effectively drugged into submission, the wound on my leg finally slowed its outward and downward spread to a halt.

I always judged the size of the wound by the size of the bandage I had to use to cover it up. At its largest I had to use two overlapping four inch by four inch gauze pads to keep it covered up. Several months after the chemo sessions were over, I woke up one morning to find that it only took one four-by-four bandage to cover the mess that was my calf. It was such an emotional moment for me that I had to do what any grown man would do in that situation. So I called my mother and told her.

She cried. I am pretty sure I did, too. I had not gone through this ordeal alone. Telling my mom that the treatment we had worked so hard to get was finally working seemed only fitting, as she and my dad had suffered right along with me every step of the way. Hey, I may act like a tough guy who does things his way, but even I know sometimes you just have to call your mommy! Later in life, being a momma's boy may have very well saved my life.

It was a good thing that the chemo was over and my wound was finally getting a bit smaller, because my life was about to go through another change. Work decided that since I had trained so many service managers within the company to do the right thing, they might as well train me to become a service manager myself. I went through part of my training in Evansville, Indiana, in an office that traditionally hated the thought of me.

Perhaps I should take a moment to expand on my job so you can better understand what most regular company employees thought of me. Many hands in a single office go into doing a termite treatment, from sales personnel, to office staff, through branch managers then service managers, and finally down to the actual treating technician. After the technician has done his job, the paperwork is then handed back to a service manager, and ultimately lands on the desk of an administrator to log everything into a computer and file the job away. If it sounds like a complicated process, well, it isn't. It is just time consuming.

It was my job to go over everything with a fine toothed comb, to look at all the hands that had touched the job and find any mistakes. If I found mistakes it was my job to report on them and then correct them. That might mean taking a contract out and having it initialed by a client, or actually going out and completely redoing a termite treatment that was done wrong. I found a lot of fraud over the years, and I am not very proud of the fact that more than one person lost their job over my word -- and work --

alone. Managers had been demoted over the results of my findings in the quality assurance department of our region, and many a career was marred because I had simply done my job.

If you were to ask my coal miner father, he would have told you his son was the company "axe man," and my dad wasn't too far off the mark.

So, as you can imagine, I was not a well-liked individual in any office I walked into. Technicians were scared of me finding mistakes, managers were afraid I would affect their annual bonuses, and administrators disliked all the extra paperwork that tended to be generated when I came to town. I worked for the same company as they did, but I most certainly wasn't an employee as far as they were concerned. I was an adversary. Everywhere I went I encountered cold shoulders, rude remarks, and more than anything else, hatred. So when I landed in the Evansville office to start my part time service manager training, life was miserable.

There is no point in telling stories about what I went through in that office, because no matter what was done to me, it was in my nature to stand up and fight back, and so that is what I did. I eventually was moved to another office at the request of Evansville management, as we couldn't seem to get along. Having the QA guy in their office that had caused them so much grief was just too much for them to handle, and they couldn't control themselves when it came to giving me a hard time. Whenever they gave me a hard time, I took off my service manager trainee hat and put on my QA hat and gave them just as hard a time.

So I got moved to another state and to another

office, this time in Owensboro, KY. I really didn't mind this post, as one of the search and rescue teams I was on was based very near here. Working in Owensboro meant I didn't have far to drive on the nights SAR-3 had training sessions.

It wasn't long before the QA part of my job once again started heating up, and Owensboro happened to be in the center of it. When I had been stationed in Lexington I'd happened to meet a service manager there by the name of Stephen Day. He was a nice enough guy, but like all service managers he kept me at a respectable distance as I was the guy known for getting people canned. When I landed in the mess in Owensboro that had to be cleaned up, I was pleasantly surprised to find my acquaintance from Lexington had moved out of his position there and had begun working for my department. Stephen Day was now on the other side of the fence, and to be quite honest, working with me was probably not one of the things he wanted to do.

Our time working together in QA sparked a friendship that lasts to this day. Stephen, his wife Tracey, and their son CJ are really great people, and Stephen and Tracey have always found a way to help take care of me when I needed them. Stephen always laughs when he talks about those days when he worked with me, because he gives the impression he was working for me. I tell him he wasn't, but he just tells me that working with me meant doing things my way, so he was working for me. Even my best friends peg me as being stubborn!

This stint of the job had all of us once again saving the company's bacon from goof-ups, and we went everywhere from the birthplace of bluegrass legend

Bill Monroe to the stomping grounds of civil war legend Sue Mundy. The work we ended up doing opened up many doors for me, and as I found the wound on my leg slowly shrinking, I found my star at work rising. I was able to start picking and choosing where I went to a certain extent, and for once in my life I wasn't staying in a hotel room every night.

I was able to see my son more, take more shifts at the fire department, and finally start to enjoy life a little bit. After all that I had been through, I thought a little of the good life was in order.

7- THE BIG LEAGUES

All my hard work had finally paid off. My life was turning into an enjoyable experience. I had always been told that real life doesn't start until you are in your thirties and I hadn't believed it, but nonetheless it is true. I was no longer struggling so hard to make a living, I enjoyed my job, and my son was now not only *my* kiddo but a small human being with thoughts, ideas, and expressions. I found more joy in my son at the age of ten than ever before, and no father could have asked for a better kid.

As I always had, I continued on with the fire department on the weekends as well as my career during the week. I had left SAR-3 and the county rescue squad had slowed down, so I found myself with time on my hands and money in my pockets for the first time in my life. For about a year I got to travel for pleasure, catch up on some hunting and fishing, and more importantly stay home. I still had the wound on my leg, but it was slowly and surely growing smaller with every bandage change. Some days I would wake up out of bed to find I could actually see a line of demarcation where new skin had grown in from the night before.

I actually got to take my son on a real vacation and I even let him choose where we went. That year we ended up in the panhandle of Florida near Saint

George Island. I still remember the look and sound of awe that came from my son when we walked over the crest of the beach for the first time and he gazed upon the Gulf of Mexico. I couldn't have paid for better planning, as not sixty yards out in the water three dolphins were jumping in the water. Yep, my first time taking my boy to the beach we got to see dolphins in the water. That was a great vacation, and I recommend Saint George Island to anyone who wants to experience Florida.

So there I was, nearly thirty-four and finally living the life I thought I was meant to live. Things couldn't have gotten any better, or so I thought.

It seems there was beginning to be a shake up within the corporate entity that was my company, and someone somewhere had decided that my regional QA office had done its job, everything had finally been fixed, and our office would no longer be needed. All of us got the phone call, and all of us were on the knife's edge. It seemed that only one of us was to be kept and promoted into the corporate office of quality assurance, and the rest of us would be turned over to the nearest branch office to work as a technician.

I was terrified of my impending fate. I had done my job so well all those years in QA that no local office would have had me, and there were people in my QA office with better credentials than mine. I was certain that my career would soon be over, turned over to the whim of some branch manager I had upset in years past that held a grudge.

I will never forget where I was when the phone call came in. I was standing outside of an office in Bowling Green, Kentucky, helping a technician fix a piece of equipment. I didn't recognize the number, but the area code told me it was someone from corporate. Here it was: the dreaded call that would seal my fate... I was already making plans for putting in resumes with other companies when the voice on the other end of the line asked me if I wanted the corporate job.

I could not believe I had gotten the job! My friend Stephen was offered a management position at a branch, and all the rest were absorbed back into regular branch offices save one man, who got a job as a technical specialist working with my old friend Tony. So I had the job, but with one very important stipulation. My territory was going to be far away from home. My one question was whether or not I would have to move, and to my relief I would not.

I was now the newest member of the corporate staff, and my working territory ranged from Minneapolis, Minnesota, to Topeka, Kansas, and everywhere in between. My home office would be in Chicago, but I would rarely ever see it. It was more prestige, more money, and a lot more driving. My only other option was working in a branch I would not be welcome in, so I took the job.

I wasn't happy about being on the road so much again, and living out of hotel rooms, but I had to do what I had to do to provide for myself and my son. Once again my title and my supervisor had changed, but not the job. I now had a totally new set of states, branches, and managers to work with and eventually upset in the course of my duties.

Of all the things I did while working for that company, the corporate job was the most enjoyable. I got to walk the streets of Lincoln, Nebraska, eat the best sushi on the planet in Topeka, and meet more than a few professional football players while eating dinner in the hotel bar across the street from the Kansas City Chiefs' stadium in Independence, Missouri. I also got to meet a new love, and found myself in a relationship once again.

I spent less than a year in that position, but I enjoyed every minute of it! Great food, good people, beautiful countryside, and many new friends and experiences happened for me out in that western territory of mine. But life catches up to us all, and being so far away from home every day takes its toll. I remember being in the back room of a Kansas City, Kansas, office when I got a call from my son's school. There was to be a meeting in the morning about some learning issues he seemed to be having, and they requested I be there around 9:00AM.

I was almost nine hours from my home, working in a new city and I had to pack up and drive back for a short notice meeting. I made the meeting, but after nine hours on the road and little sleep, I knew I couldn't do that very often. After the meeting was over I even had to turn right around and head back to Kansas.

Between simply being a father and the untold lunacies involved with trying to maintain what was essentially a long-distance relationship, I had to contemplate the unthinkable: giving up on the challenge of the job. Honestly, it was a no-brainer. The office closest to my home was eight hours away, and the furthest was thirteen. It was too much for anyone to keep up for very long, and so I talked to my boss about options. While he didn't want to see me leave, he also understood the family pressures I was under. He found me a branch position in literally the only office I had never had any contact with in Jasper, Indiana.

That office was three hours from my house but it was doable. I had been driving all over the country working for years, so a three hour drive was nothing. All that service manager training I had been forced to endure several years before had finally paid off. I was now the newest service manager to grace the halls of the Jasper office.

I was only in my new position a few months when the relationship I was in turned rather caustic, and she and I parted company. It seemed a shame at the time, as that relationship was a good part of the reason why I had left my corporate dream job. But hind-sight is always 20-20, and it was the best thing that could have happened to me at the time. Some things aren't meant to be, and some things never should have been, a wise man once said.

My new boss was a regional manager who had great faith in my ability to fix things, so my new-found single status was very much a blessing because I was quickly put to work. My job was supposed to be running the Jasper service department employees, but I often found myself being sent to other offices to once again fix someone else's mistakes. It was some of the hardest work I had ever done, but the pay was well worth it.

Being once again close to home and single I was able to pick up a few new hobbies. One of those things happened to be Jiu Jitsu. I had the chance to catch up with an old wrestling buddy from my high school days, and he had to tell me all about this new stuff he was doing and how it was so much like rolling out the mats and wrestling for our old coach, Roy "Cherry Bomb" Cherry. "This guy loves training ex-wrestlers" was all I needed to hear. Having a lot more free time on my hands in those days, I decided to give it a try.

Getting on that mat for the first time and learning what Jiu Jitsu was from Sensei Eric Myers was an eye opener. It was so much like - and also unlike - wrestling that I fell in love with it immediately. It simply hit all my buttons. Jiu Jitsu is exercise, friendship, challenges, and fun all rolled into one art. I was so out of shape when I started that it wasn't even funny. I had spent the better part of fourteen years riding around in a company truck, eating out of drive-thru sacks, and smoking off and on. Those first few weeks were torture, but it was a torture I gladly accepted because Jiu Jitsu was something I truly needed in my life then.

All of the stresses of work, fatherhood, failed relationships, and illness I got to put on the mat and arm-bar into submission. I spent close to a year on Eric's mats before work once again moved me, and that year put me into the best shape of my life since my senior year of high school. I achieved a third belt ranking in the Nihon Ryu Jiu Jitsu, which was at the time taught at Myers Dojo, and every time I tied on that belt it was a reminder to myself that no matter what life threw at me I was tough enough to beat any problem into submission.

8 - TRANSITION

Nothing in my life ever seems to stay static, especially when it comes to work. Jasper didn't last very long before I was asked to move into a different position once again. I was now headed to Evansville, not the office I had once dreaded, but a new one. I had ended up in that old adversarial office quite often to help them out while working for Jasper, and had actually managed to make a few friends there in the process.

The first person in that office to decide I wasn't a total ass was Tara Hickman. She was an absolute spitfire of a woman who took crap off of exactly zero people. I think she first became my friend just to irritate other people in her office. I still remember her dragging me along to the Evansville office Christmas party. That was such a fun night! My reputation with those people was that of a complete asshole, and I think many were absolutely dumbfounded to discover I might actually be a decent human being. Tara was kind enough to include me in all kinds of shenanigans, and I had more fun hanging out with that woman than any man has a right to have.

Becoming Tara's friend paved the way for the next transition of my career, into a new Evansville office. It would be way too boring to try an explain it all, but in a nutshell, some corporate bean-counter thought it would be a great idea to take all the pest control technicians out of one office and stick them in another. In the infinite wisdom of my regional manager, he decides to put me in there when the little pest control office wasn't performing. To this day I have no idea why they decided to pull me out of my then comfortable position in Jasper, where things were beginning to run smoothly.

I was told to go, so I went. I was given the title of branch manager without the pay, but with all the headaches. It was a doomed venture from the start, separating pest control operations from the termite control operations, but that wasn't my call. I will say that my little office was the only office out of all the splits that actually hit their goals and made their numbers. Oh, wait, now I know why I was sent there... apparently they thought I could fix anything and make it work. My saving grace was that my friend Tara got to come with me and be my administrator.

One of the things I was told I had to do at that time was move closer to my office. In all my years with that company I had never been asked to move away from my hometown, I had always been able to drive in to work no matter how far away. My home that I had bought so long ago had begun to build up a lot of memories of pain and suffering, and being a fourteen room two story house it had become rather large for only my son and me.

At about the same time that I had begun working in Jasper there had been a regime change of sorts in my small town, and the new mayor decided that the part time fire fighters were no longer a necessity, so my shifts at the department had been cut back to nothing. One evening I went in to cover a holiday shift for a full time guy to find out the part-timers were no longer allowed to take shifts. Just like that I was back to being a volunteer. But I didn't really mind, as it was never about the pay, anyway.

No longer being so urgently needed at the fire department was the clinch for my decision as I prepared to sell my home and move closer to my job in Indiana. The move was very much an eye-opener for me, as I had to figure out how to take fourteen rooms of house and condense them into a one bedroom condo. That was what I ended up settling into right across the river from Evansville in the city of Henderson, KY. I did manage to do it, simply by pitching more things than I kept. I learned something about myself in the process of it all - I really enjoyed living in small spaces.

I had grown up in a sprawling hundred year old house with lots of room, and that is much the same type of house I ended up buying for myself and my second wife. Going from that big house to my little condo was a joy. Small spaces are easy to keep clean, inexpensive to heat and cool, and very cheap to lease. I think the next home I own will have to be just about the size of that condo I had. It was just perfect for my needs.

It wasn't long after I moved that I realized I knew no one at all except my employees and Tara. That didn't last long, though. Taking over that little pest control office put me right in the face of many people who had heard of my reputation as a hard-nosed son of a bitch, but never got to see it for themselves. I like to think that I changed the opinions of a lot of people in that small time that I ran that office. Many of the people that worked for me learned that although I am hard headed and stubborn, I am really not all that bad a person to work for or get to know.

One of the pest control techs that ended up working for me was a young lady named Jenny. I don't think she would ever admit it now, but in the beginning I think she disliked me immensely. I can't really blame her, I mean, I am a self-proclaimed asshole, after all, but eventually she came around.

Tara would drag me out to all the after hour hang outs, and that is where I got to meet some of my best and most dear friends. Jenny has a very great family of brothers, sisters, in-laws, her mother, and the love of her life, Bob. I spent many a Saturday night hanging around on the outside edges of this tight-knit group at a little bar called the Marigold. I think the thing that really brought me into the group was my love for karaoke and my willingness to sing. Really, who can hate a guy willing to make a fool of himself in a bar filled with drunks?

Work, as always, changed on me. The bean-counters had decided their great idea of a split was a bad idea after all, and I was sent back to Jasper for all of a week. It seems that the split with the termite control office had brought to light some disturbing financial numbers, and they had to let someone go. Now who do you think it was they decided to send down there and fix the new mess? It seems I was moving offices and jobs once again. I was sent right into the middle of the viper pit I had tried so diligently to stay out of. I was now the service manager of the Evansville office.

All my employees from the split followed me back, and I ended up with between twenty-five and thirty employees to deal with on a daily basis. One morning not long after I had taken over that dreaded office I woke up to find that there was finally nothing left of the wound under the bandage on my calf. I was truly in disbelief, and I went for several weeks with the distinct feeling that I had lost or forgotten something. In reality, I had. I changed the bandage on my leg for the better part of three and a half years, and nearly a year after I had finished my chemotherapy my leg had finally healed.

I ended up with a half grapefruit sized hole in my leg I could stick my fist into, courtesy of my Behcet's Disease. During all that time my symptoms had never gone away, but they had become so much a part of my daily life that I really didn't think about the pain. If I got an ulcer in my mouth, I talked and ate around it. If I got a small BD wound on my skin I bandaged it and went on. That was the real gift of that horrible calf wound. It had hurt so much and taken up so much of my life that the little things simply didn't matter anymore. Think about that wound for a moment. Imagine it being on your leg. Imagine looking at a hole in your body every day for three and a half years, and changing bandages twice a day for that length of time.

My only options were to grit my teeth and power through it, or go insane. I chose to deal with it, face it head on, and conquer the pain and suffering. I chose to own it, and I did for more than three years. After dealing with that, anything I could imagine happening to me was chump change. I would eventually find out there were tougher things in life than that fist sized chunk of my leg dying away, but not yet. Behcet's didn't whip my ass, it never has, and it never will. My learning to fight all battles when I was a teenager -

and the reason I had to learn to never back down - had served me well in that fight with BD.

With a healed leg, a new home, new job, and now a few friends, my life started to look up once again. I was missing the Jiu Jitsu mat and fighting fires, but not everything in this new life could be perfect. I was no longer sitting on the outside of this small tight-knit group of folks. I had been accepted as a human being, and more importantly, as a friend. I have to say, when you are accepted as a friend of the Luttrell clan, you are also accepted as part of the family. I had found friends in Jenny, Bob, and the rest of the family that I will never forget.

I had an administrator in my new office, and her family also hung out quite a bit with Jenny and Bob. Rayetta was a ball of fire, and her fiancé Mike and I became good friends. He introduced me to the horrible game of golf, and Mike, Bob, and I spent many a Sunday afternoon playing eighteen holes of pure frustration while buying beer from the cart girls who drove around the links.

Raye-Raye's family also took me as a friend, and I always had such a great time when I hung out with them. In those early days in that Evansville office I don't think I would have made it through without Tara, the Luttrell clan, and the Stuckey family. Tara is gone from us now, but I am quite sure wherever she may be she knows how much her friendship meant to me. To the Lutrells and Stuckeys I say thank you.... Your love, friendship, and kindness kept me happy and sane during a very rough time in my life. It wasn't just me, either. Those great people took in my son as well. Whenever he was with me he was made to feel welcome and wanted. You are all great people.

I ended up making another great friend during my time in Evansville. When you run a business that involves frequent trips into the crawl spaces of houses, having a skinny guy on the payroll is a plus. Eric Kimbrough was that skinny guy on my payroll and from my very first day in that office I made it *my* job to keep him happy. I think he was none too happy with being suddenly in the QA guy's spotlight, but I needed someone who was small enough to do the job, and willing to do it my way. Kimbrough was both of those things.

I remember buying him lunch not long after I became his boss and having a very candid conversation with him about who I was and who I wasn't. All this guy had ever heard about me was that I was the man that made people lose their jobs, and I was a jerk in the process. We came to an agreement that day that I would do everything I could to keep him in work as long as he would give me the opportunity to prove I was not the axe-man everyone claimed I was.

Little did I know at the time, Eric could have cared less about my reputation in the company. He was a gulf war veteran and a retired Army MP. He could smell bullshit a mile away, and didn't put much stock in what other people said. I also bought him lunch, that didn't hurt my cause either. Kimbrough has actually told me that. I worked Eric harder than I have ever worked any other employee, but I never worked him any harder than I worked myself. The unfortunate truth was that I had inherited $100,000 worth of errors and fraudulent work when I came to that office. Kimbrough and I were the ones that had to clean it up. And we did.

Somewhere in the midst of all that hard work mutual respect was gained, and a true friendship was forged. It wasn't long before Eric started coming around for the weekend parties with my other friends, and I in turn would bring my son and hang out with Eric, his girlfriend, and their kids. My son even dated his daughter. Did I mention Kimbrough was a veteran? We spent a lot of time on the weekends going to shooting ranges and putting rounds downrange, and I reminded my son of this fact more than once. My boy still dated his daughter, and him still being alive today is a testament to my ability to raise a gentleman.

My friendship with Eric ended up rekindling an old passion I had from much earlier in life. Before I met my first wife I owned a motorcycle, and I loved that old bike. It was a 1973 Honda CB750-Four, and it would flat out scream. When I first bought it the engine wouldn't even turn over, and I tinkered with it forever. I ended up getting it started late one winter night sitting in the kitchen of a little place I rented with a buddy. He and his girlfriend were sound asleep in his bedroom in this tiny single wide trailer while I was kick-starting the bike in the kitchen.

After cleaning out the carburetors for perhaps the hundredth time, the bike finally decided to crank and run. In the dead of winter, in the kitchen of a little trailer, with my buddy and his girl asleep right down the hall. It cranked up, it was loud, it spit exhaust fumes everywhere, and I think I scared them both out of a year of their life, but the damned thing started!

That was the beginning of my love affair with motorcycles. I kept that bike until I married my kiddo's mom and she said it had to go, so it went.

Over the years I had stopped so many times to look at motorcycles for sale, and it was either not the right time in my life, or it was and I just didn't have the money to spare.

By the time I met my friend Eric, I had both the time and the money, so I bought a bike. Actually, I bought his bike. He had this beautiful Suzuki sitting in his garage that he had bought, rode one time, and then put it up on its belly stand. I have not known that man to be afraid of much of anything, but that bike had scared him when he took off on it. Of course, there were only two things I was afraid of, and that bike wasn't one of them. It took one test ride of that bike and I was in love with motorcycles all over again.

I bought that old GS650 from Kimbrough and he turned around and bought a Honda cruiser. Apparently Honda Shadows aren't nearly as scary to ride as a Suzuki GS650G. I have ridden that Honda of his, and let me tell you it ain't a bike, it's a boat, and I get a bit nervous on that big fat bike. To each his own, I guess.

Around the same time I got the bike I decided I missed doing rescue work, and I applied to and joined the Henderson City/County Rescue Squad. Of all the departments I have been a part of that has to be one of my favorites. HCCRS has the distinction of being the only extraction crew outside of the city limits of Henderson in the entire county. If there was an automotive accident that required Jaws of Life, anywhere in the county, HCCRS was called.

That squad also handled all water rescue for the county, and with both the Green and Ohio rivers, we were kept on our toes. The squad was run by Bryant

Woodard and Bryan Coghill, and all volunteer or not, it was the most professional department I have ever had the pleasure of serving on. Throughout all the search and rescue ops, all the water rescue runs, and all those extractions, Woodard and the entire Coghill clan kept the place running like a well-oiled machine. I can't say enough about that great group of volunteers that I worked with during my time living in Henderson.

I spent my weekdays working, some of my weeknights once again answering pager tones for rescue runs, and my weekends riding motorcycles and hanging out with my friends. I still kept in touch and occasionally saw the rest of my friends I had made along the way, like Matthew and Stephen in Lexington, or all my old friends back home in Providence, but most of my time was spent at my new job and my new home.

I had some of the best times of my adult life during those days in Evansville, but as with all things, times change and so does my job. I had lived in Henderson for nearly two years when once again my company wanted me elsewhere. This time, however it wasn't something somewhere that needed to be fixed, this time I was the problem.

The very regional manager that had hired me in to fix so many of the problems in Indiana started doing shady things himself. He was asking all of us to break the law to get work done, but morals, pride, and credentials got in the way of me complying. Earlier in the year I had applied to take, and then passed a very important test. I had become a certified entomologist, and had passed the test on working skill and knowledge alone. I didn't have a college degree, so even being allowed to take the test was a challenge.

One of the things required of a certified entomologist is something of a pledge to always do your work the right and proper way. That wasn't a problem for me, as I had been working that way my entire career. So, when our regional manager decided we needed to start doing things the wrong way so he could pad his bonus, alarm bells went off for me. I began to discreetly make phone calls to both people within the company and state agencies involved with chemical application in Indiana. I had not worked hard all my life to be dragged down by a money hungry boss, so I was taking steps.

It is unfortunate that he made sure his whistleblower in the Evansville office was gone before he himself was removed, but such is life. If I had to do it all over again, I would. I was taught from an early age that you never let anyone compromise your morals, no matter the cause. So I did what I thought was right while putting myself out of a job. In the end it all worked out, because my long-time friend Stephen Day was running the office down in Bowling Green, and he wanted me to come work for him. So that's what I did. I was barely in Bowling Green a month when I got word that my old regional manager had been demoted and sent to Pittsburgh to work in a branch office. Couldn't have happened to a nicer guy.

It was during the ice storm of 2009 that I packed my things and once again moved work. I had no idea that in a little more than a year's time my life would be irrevocably changed.

9 - A SORE THROAT

Bowling Green was an entirely new experience for me. It had been at least twelve years since I had been a normal, every-day employee within the company. My only responsibilities were to my tiny portion of the office, and being responsible for just my own actions was rather refreshing.

No one else in the office seemed to know what to do with me. Here I was, the company axe man, drinking the same coffee from the same pot, sitting in at office meetings like everyone else, and taking orders instead of giving them. I think a lot of the people I worked with thought I was some kind of plant, put there by a suspicious corporate someone to spy on the regular employees. I simply went about my normal routine, doing what I was told to do, and generally working my ass off.

Being low man on the totem pole had its advantages. I didn't go home at night and worry about bottom lines, sales targets, quarterly bonuses, or state inspectors. All I worried about was doing my ordinary job and making a paycheck. When Stephen asked me for my help or expertise I gave it, but running the whole office was no longer something I had to do.

Bowling Green itself is a fine place to live, and I did enjoy all that there was to do there. There are race tracks, theme parks, fine restaurants, and of course

Western Kentucky University. You are just a quick jaunt down the road from Mammoth Cave, and Nashville is only about an hour's drive down I-65. Living there put me many miles from my family, friends, and my son, but I still enjoyed it.

Now that the weight of a branch wasn't on my shoulders I found more time to ride my motorcycle, and the roads in south central Kentucky were made for two wheels. Every moment I wasn't in a uniform for work I was out on my bike. Behcet's, of course, was still my constant companion, but I had trained myself to push the pain somewhere down so deep that I honestly can't remember any truly bad episodes with BD the entire time I was there.

I still occasionally got to see my friends from Indiana and from back home if I went to see them, and even more rarely I could get my friends to come to me. During the late summer of 2010, my friend Kimbrough rode his motorcycle down from his mother's place in Lexington where he was living at the time. That weekend we put close to eight hundred miles on our bikes riding from south central Kentucky all the way to Lexington. We took the back roads on the way back, Eric riding with me part of the way. We rode back through historic Danville and Perryville, Kentucky, and we parted ways under the huge old Osage tree at Fort Harrod. I rode the rest of the way back by myself, reveling in the simple joy of the wind in my face, the sun on my back, and the landscape sliding by as I straightened curves and flattened hills on my 'Zuki. That would be the last real ride I ever took on that bike, and I am glad that ride back to Bowling Green was such a beautiful one.

My one true friend there in Bowling Green was my

boss, and we hung out whenever he was in town. Stephen ran two offices, one in Bowling Green, and one in Somerset, KY. On the days he spent down my way he would mostly stay in a hotel. We ate out a lot, always striving to find the better place to go, or the cooler atmosphere to be in. Working for a regular branch meant taking a large pay cut, and for the first time in a long time money was tight for me. Many a night I would have stayed home because I couldn't afford to eat out, but Stephen took care of me. He did a lot for me while I lived there and worked for him, and I will never be able to thank him enough for the chances he took to hire me on and help me out.

About a year after I arrived in Bowling Green Stephen and his wife Tracey were blessed with a son. I stood on the sidelines and watched as this courageous couple fought every obstacle to reach out from across the world and bring home their adopted son. The look on his face every time he showed off a new picture the agency had sent him was priceless. Stephen and Tracey had tried the old-fashioned way and had been unable to conceive. This little boy was the answer to their prayers.

Not long after Stephen and Tracey brought home their son, my friend and co-worker of so many years and offices left the company, in search of greener pastures. I had myself been looking, and at very close to the same time had found a new direction in life. After seventeen years in the pest control industry, I had decided to go back to school. I was going to become a nurse. I had found a school in Nashville, close to my older brother that was willing to accept me into their nursing program with a scholarship.

This was a very scary proposition for me. This was

to be a total turnaround from everything I had ever done before, and leaving behind a seventeen year career to return to school was enough to frighten anyone a bit. I needed a change, though, so I decided to go for it. Every challenge in life I had experienced I had stood up and fought head on, never backing down. Nursing school was simply going to be a new challenge to overcome, so right after my thirty-seventh birthday in mid-summer of 2010, I signed my final paperwork with the school and prepared my letter of resignation to the company I had known for so long.

Being as Stephen was gone I had to address the letter to the service manager, Dennis Fulton, and the regional manager - my old friend and boss - Damon Bayens. I found it interesting that my career had come full circle. I had started my time in the company with Damon, and after doing so many things and going so many places, here I was once again with the retired jarhead when I was ready to leave the company forever.

I really hated leaving Dennis hanging, as filling Stephen Day's shoes was a tough job for anyone, but he understood my need to move on in my life. We always talked about you dragging out your bike and you and I going for a ride, Dennis. We still need to do that sometime.

I had planned my resignation for October the 15th, 2010, and I gave Dennis and Damon about a month's notice sometime in September. It was about the same time that I noticed a little tickle in the back of my throat. This didn't worry me much. As many times before, Behcet's had seen fit to put an ulcer in my throat, and early fall was always the worse time for my BD attacks. I had dealt with it before, and I would deal with it again.

It was only a few days later that I realized this might not be a BD attack, and I was simply getting sick. So, off a local doctor's office I went. The young nurse practitioner diagnosed me with - of all things - a yeast infection in my throat with possible bronchitis, and she sent me out with a prescription for antibiotics and a warning to get some rest. The antibiotic I took, but rest I did not. I still had a job to do and a paycheck to earn. Less than a week after that first tickle in my throat, I was lying on my couch in my little apartment in Bowling Green feeling like death warmed over.

I had felt so bad that I called in sick to work, and being as I was totally alone and feeling very sick I did what any grown man in my situation would do - I called my mother and asked her to come get me. If I had to be off work sick, I might as well be sick on mom and dad's couch at their house. That decision undoubtedly saved my life.

Mom drove over a hundred miles one way to come pick up her sick kid, and she brought me home to take care of me. That very day I had gone back to the doctor and had been given a new diagnosis of strep, and a prescription for different antibiotics. We went through a pharmacy drive through on the way out of town, and I haven't been back to that town since my mother drove us out on September 21st, 2010.

I laid on her couch feeling worse and worse for a couple of days before we decided I needed to see a doctor again, and quick. I had gotten to the point that I couldn't breathe and my throat hurt so badly that I couldn't even swallow. I was in horrible pain and I was becoming more dehydrated by the moment. My mother piled me into the truck and we headed to the ER of Regional Medical Center in Madisonville. It was the evening of Friday, September 24th, and I ended up being released from that ER early the next morning.

I don't remember very much about that night, except for having an IV in my arm and being given pain medication. The thing I remember the most is being able to swallow after they put something through the IV port. I know now that this ER visit was the beginning of the end for me. The ER doctor never spent more than a moment or two with me, and I am truly convinced that if he had done his job properly my life might be very different right now.

I know that he diagnosed me with thrush, but only because I made a post about it on Facebook, and many months later I found the post that I don't even remember writing.

"I was told I had a case of old fashioned thrush......So, I went through 4 bags of IV fluids, 2 dilaudid/zofran combo shots, steroid shots and other things while in the hospital..... I was rolled out to the truck in a wheel chair, new pain meds script in hand and a vile mouthwash for thrush as well."

There were even some responses on that post from friends wishing me a speedy recovery, but I don't remember any of it. I really remember only two things after that night in the ER. I remember sitting at the table with my brother and sister-in-law playing a hand of euchre, and I remember a simple glimpse of a small, green oxygen bottle. That is all that I remember, so everything else after I had to be told about later.

My brother Kyle and his significant other Kim were in town for the weekend, as we were celebrating his birthday. At some point during that weekend I felt well enough to get up and play a few games of euchre, and then I went back and lay down on the couch. Apparently after I laid back down I didn't get up again for an entire day, and my family really began to worry about me.

Four days after I was released from the ER, I am told I staggered into the kitchen from the living room where I had been sleeping and dropped into a chair, whispering "I need help."

I don't know who all was there, and I don't know what they said in response to me, but I do know that I was somehow gotten into a vehicle and someone took me down to the very fire department and ambulance service that I had served for years. To this day I am unsure which of my old colleagues were working that night and saw me in such a sorry state.

I do know that they wanted to get me in the ambulance and take me right then and there to the emergency room, but I must have refused. Knowing me I probably did, as I don't know an EMT or paramedic out there that would willingly ride in the back as a patient instead of as the technician.

My breathing must have been impeded enough to concern them all because they gave my parents oxygen, a line, and a mask for me to use as my folks took me on to the hospital. My mother tells me that I didn't want the mask on my face, and I think that for the next month after I would continue trying to take masks away from my mouth and nose. I don't know the reactions I may have gotten as I was helped into the ER that night, but I do know I was very quickly taken into a treatment room.

The attending doctor that night was a young resident by the name of Joshua Kitchens, and he is the doctor that examined me. It was decided that I needed to be taken directly to the intensive care unit, and a team rushed me 150 yards or so through the maze of hospital hallways to get me there. I would spend the next three weeks in that semi-circular section of the hospital, barely clinging to life, and continually fighting.

Long after, I found out that at some point during that dash to the ICU my body had had enough and decided to give up the ghost. Later I asked my mother if I had ever come close to dying during the entire ordeal, and she broke down in tears when I asked. She had apparently wanted to save me from ever having to know, or save herself from ever having to tell me, but when I asked she told me the truth. Doctor Kitchens didn't think I would make that short trip down the hall to ICU, and that is why they took me there at a run. At some point before I reached ICU I am told I died, and people worked very hard to bring me back.

I arrived in the ICU sometime after midnight on the morning September 29th, 2010. That is the night I died and was brought back to life, and that was also the last night I would ever feel the ground beneath the feet I was born with.

PART TWO

10 - THE HARD FIGHT

The next three weeks of my life would be spent in a coma. Much of that time I was trapped in my own little world inside my head, living a bizarre life filled with frightening things. I know nothing about my treatments and the touch-and-go moments, save what I have been told by my family and care staff. Anything you read here about what was done to keep me on this earth is all second-hand information, but I will try to relay it as completely as I can nonetheless.

What ended up making me so sick and nearly killing me was a MRSA bacterial infection. What that very first nurse practitioner in Bowling Green had thought was a yeast infection was actually a bacterial infection in my throat. We have no idea how it got there, or started, but that is what it was. MRSA is a very common thing, it can be found anywhere. It is often found even on the surface of our skin.

At work I shook a lot of hands and touched a lot of doorknobs. I also crawled in some of the nastiest crawlspaces in existence. You would be surprised about all the nasty things that can exist under your home, but I would not. I have seen it all. I was a constant hand washer because of the people and things I came into contact with on the job, but it only takes one moment of forgetfulness to let something like this happen.

I was smoking while living in Bowling Green, so there is a very real possibility that I came into contact with MRSA on a job site and then transferred it from hand to mouth while lighting up a cigarette. That is one possibility. It could have been something else entirely, but we will never know.

What we do know is that the infection spread from my throat to my lungs, causing the bronchitis symptoms, and then from my lungs to my blood stream, causing sepsis. I get asked often by total strangers how I lost my legs, and telling them "I got a sore throat" always gets me long stares, but that was the ultimate cause of all my problems. I had been misdiagnosed so many times that when it was finally determined what the real problem was, it was simply too late, as I had gone septic.

I do want to make it quite clear that Behcet's Disease had nothing to do with the loss of my legs. Many people that know me assumed it was the BD, but it was not. It was simply bad luck. It could have happened to anyone. I find it ironic at times that a fire fighter who has crawled into many a fully involved structure, who has cut open more cars on the roadside extracting victims, and who has spent more time hanging off the sides of perfectly good buildings doing rescue rappel training would lose limbs because of a sore throat. That's not to mention the many thousands of miles I have put in riding motorcycles helmet-less, or the - literally - million plus miles I have logged driving over the years for a pest control company. None of that, oh no. It was a "cough-cough, I need a lozenge" sore-freaking-throat.

Think about that the next time you get a tickle in

the back of your throat and pop a Ricola in your mouth.

My body had become so full of infection it had begun to shut down, and that is what the doctors and nurses had to fight on an hourly basis as I lay in that hospital bed in a comatose state. I, of course, knew nothing of what was going on. I was living in a schizophrenic fantasy land my own mind had made for me. I am told that many people live another life inside their head while in a coma, and I hope for their sake they lived a better one than what my tortured psyche provided.

I spent much of my time believing that I was being held prisoner by someone. I wasn't sure who, because my captors kept changing. Knowing what I know now, I realize that I must have had some lucid moments while I was in ICU, because I would recognize several of my captors when I finally woke up. I spent much of my time believing I was being held captive in the back room of a Chinese restaurant. I was strapped down between boxes of fortune cookies, and I couldn't move.

Occasionally I would hear my captor talking, but I couldn't understand the words, and sometimes that devious Chinese cook would bring others around to take a peek at the poor guy locked up in the back room. I got the distinct impression that I would be butchered and served to the restaurant patrons out front, and I was terrified. I would try and plan my escape, but every time I tried to get up I found that my most private of parts had been chained down. I couldn't move.

I was horrified to find that I was chained to the floor by my crotch. In my mind, I was there for months, never being fed, always so cold, and no one ever coming to even talk to me. Occasionally I would dream while in that little back room, and when I did I found myself riding along in the cab of a semi-tractor with a beautiful blonde driver.

She would come and get me and we would drive all over the countryside and she would tell me about where we were going, and what we were hauling in the trailer being pulled behind us. She eventually stopped coming to see me, and that made me so sad. All I had left now was the cold floor I was being held captive on, and it was getting colder all the time. I had lost all the feeling in my feet. I saw my truck-driving savior months later after I came home from the hospital, and I was shocked and relieved to finally realize where she had come from. I was catching up with episodes of Ice Road Truckers on Netflix when I saw driver Lisa Kelly and recognized her from my warped dreams. Apparently the television had been playing IRT in my ICU room and I had incorporated her into my coma dreams.

Have you ever seen the movie "Sixteen Candles"? It came out in the eighties, and it was a major hit for the time. Molly Ringwald had never looked better, and Jon Cryer played the role of a lifetime as Molly's geek friend called Ducky. I bring this up because after I stopped thinking I was in the back store room of a restaurant, I thought I was in a slaughterhouse being tormented by Ducky. Crazy, I know, but the mind does strange things when the body is in a comatose state.

Ducky always left me lying on a table unable to move. It was very bright, it smelled funny, and there always seemed to be conveyor belts running with slabs of meat on them. I would sit for hours and watch sides of beef riding along to some unknown destination, and I would occasionally reach out to try and touch them as they passed close by, but I just couldn't move my arms.

The table I was forced to lay on was a stainless steel job like you might find in a grocery store butcher shop. I was in constant fear of the butcher showing up, because I just knew if he did I would be cut up into pieces. That was my constant fear. I was going to be chopped up and fed to some unwitting person who thought they were eating sweet-and-sour chicken. I did not want to be deep fried and drizzled in sauce, and I knew that was Ducky's plans for me.

I was in constant pain, and somewhere in my addled brain I knew that in reality I must be on death's door. Every time Ducky would come see me, all I could hear him say was that I could make the pain stop if I wanted, it was my choice. Right beside my table was my own conveyor belt, and it rose way up on a slant toward the ceiling. At the top was a hole where anything riding would be dumped. I somehow knew that anything that went that way would die.

So that was my choice, every time Ducky came to torture me with words. "You can make it stop. All you have to do is take a ride. It will all be over then." I didn't want to take that ride, I didn't want to die, I wanted the hell out of this strange place where I couldn't move and everything was so frightening. Every day for what felt like years he came, offering the same way out, and all the time I was hurting worse and worse, losing more and more of myself.

Finally the day came when I was offered that way

out from all the pain, and to my shame I took it. I finally said *yes*. I knew what it meant to be put on that belt, but in a moment of weakness I chose the easy way out. Riding up that conveyor belt meant no more pain, no more suffering, and no more fear, but it also meant I was giving up and letting them kill me. I wasn't halfway up the belt when I began screaming, telling them I didn't want to die, telling them that I wanted off, but no one listened to me, they just let me ride up and up until the conveyor belt dumped me through the hole.

I don't remember anything after that until I had my first real memory after waking from the coma. To this day I am still ashamed of myself for breaking down and being weak, and accepting that ride up the belt. I have never given up on anything in my life and coma-nightmare or not, I gave up and quit for a moment.

While I was having several years' worth of adventures in wacko-land, my doctors and nurses were thinking way outside of the box to try and keep me alive during my nearly three week coma. One of my biggest problems aside from the sepsis was that my blood pressure had dropped to around 36/30. The average human BP is right around 120/80, and mine was quite a bit lower than average. I have a naturally low BP to begin with, and on a good day mine will be in the neighborhood of 90/60, so that worked in my favor. My body was used to working at lower pressure levels, and I had in fact once been a walking, talking, functioning human being with a BP of 56/40. If you're not in the medical field this may not seem like much, but those that are know better. That's just who I am, I refuse to quit.

Along with the low BP problems came organ failure. The organs in my body were deciding to call it quits. I had a cocktail of major antibacterial medications being pumped into me trying to kill out the MRSA, but it was everywhere in my system because of the blood sepsis.

Before I go any further I feel I need to make it clear what exactly my prognosis was; I was going to die. According to the doctors, no matter what they did, I was probably going to die at any moment anyway. They told my family this, point blank. Every time someone came into the ICU waiting room to talk to my family, they expected to hear that I had finally expired. So really, it didn't matter what wild or crazy treatments the doctors tried, I was a dead man anyway. Sounds a bit cavalier, I know.

The fact that I was expected not to make it liberated Dr. Kitchens from the need to hold back. Anything and everything could be tried, because I was either going to die or I wasn't. They had to come up with some way to get rid of the infection faster than with simple medications. Dr. Kitchens' unconventional thinking led him to the bright idea of cleaning out the source of the sepsis: my blood.

He went to my family and asked if he could try to use a dialysis machine to scrub the infection out of my blood. If it worked, I might have more of a fighting chance to beat the MRSA, but with a blood pressure riding in the 30's, putting me on the machine could very well kill me. To my folks it didn't matter. If they didn't try it I was going to die - if they did try it I might have a better prognosis. So the order was made and the machine was brought in.

After the procedure was over my parents were told

the news; I had taken the dialysis without the tiniest hiccup, and everyone taking care of me was a bit amazed. My BP had not wavered, and the dialysis had helped clear the infection from my blood. "He is a fighter," they said. "He wants to live," they told my parents, and my family gained the smallest bit of hope.

I don't know who all was in the waiting room or in the room with me while I was in my coma, but I know that at some point both my brothers, my parents, and my son were all in attendance. When decisions had to be made, they all made them, and the patent answer was "whatever you have to do to keep Neil alive." No matter what treatments I was given, I kept fighting. I am told that those words were on everyone's lips. "He keeps fighting, he wants to live."

Even with dialysis and the antibacterial drugs, the infection had yet to be controlled, and my blood pressure was an ongoing problem. My major organs were being starved for oxygen, and while the tube down my throat keeping me breathing could pump all the oxygen it wanted into my lungs, if the blood wasn't flowing, the organs were going to perish. This became the major concern. Brain damage was often discussed, and my family was warned that it was a very real possibility that if I did wake up, I might not be the same.

My blood pressure was very low, but it was steady. The sepsis that was ravaging my body was going to kill me, and something had to be done. There was a controversial medication on the market made specifically for cases such as mine, but it had its dangers. It was discussed with my family, and the immediate answer was the same: "keep Neil alive."

The medication was called Xigris, and could not be used by Dr. Kitchens until the every single department head in the hospital had signed off on it. Using this medication meant dire things for me. Even if it killed the infection coursing through my body, it could very likely make me bleed out. My blood pressure could drop, and the only way to raise my BP again would be to starve my extremities of life-giving oxygen to keep my core alive. If they used it, it was very likely that if I did survive, I would lose my arms and my legs. I would become an amputee.

My family made the decision for me and gave the go-ahead for the treatment. The department heads gave their signatures and Dr. Kitchens gave me Xigris in my IV drip.

11 - SHOVEL FACE

I am sure I saw quite a few things when I awoke from the coma, but I don't really remember anything visual from that time. I had figured out that I was in the hospital, but I didn't know why. My most pressing concern was the frigidly cold and horribly heavy wet boots that I felt strapped to both my feet.

They were on so tight that I couldn't move my lower legs, and the fluid chill made me miserable. Obviously, something was wrong with my feet and the boots were some part of the treatment. I remember being very frustrated that I couldn't kick them off, and it hurt like hell every time I tried.

The other thing that was a constant concern to me was the breathing tube sticking down my throat. It was uncomfortable and it made me breathe on someone else's schedule rather than my own. I immediately rebelled against it, but I couldn't seem to get my hands to work well enough to get the whole apparatus away from my face. I am told that throughout my time in the coma I tried to take the thing off my face, and it finally took my father telling me rather sternly that I needed it to breathe so leave it alone. Even in a coma I did what my old man told me to do, and I left the breathing mask and tube alone.

I don't know how long I was awake before someone noticed, but it could not have been long. I spent most of my time sleeping, and when I was awake I was trying to get the boots off my feet. How long I spent awake without vision is a mystery to me, but I do remember vividly the first thing I actually saw when my vision returned. It was my son, and he was wearing a shovel on his face.

I know now that he was wearing a hospital mask to protect both himself and me from infection, but at the time I thought my son was wearing a pink and white striped spade shovel over the lower half of his face, and I found that extremely funny. I didn't understand it, but I thought it was funny nonetheless. It was also a very emotional thing for me. I couldn't understand what was going on, but I knew that I was in the hospital - obviously in bad shape - and I was looking at my son. I cried. I cried and sobbed as best I could with that tube down my throat, because there was my son. I didn't know anything else but that my baby boy, the best thing I had ever done in my life, was there beside me. I was hurting, confused, and still mostly hallucinating from the after-effects of the coma, but my son was there, so it was going to be ok.

After all the nightmares I had lived through in that horrible coma-life, my son was with me now, and seeing him made me so happy I cried.

Everything else I saw from that moment forward was simple flashes of reality, spaced between hallucinations and drug induced sleep. The only time I seemed to be able to focus in on reality is when another shovel covered face would float up out of the mists to look at me. I remember seeing my friends Jenny, Bob, and Kimbrough, as well as my parents, and of course my son returned often. Sometimes they talked to me, but I couldn't understand the words they were saying. The expressions on their faces spoke to me in volumes, though. It was the looks in the eyes of all those shovel-faces that made me understand that something really bad had happened to me, and I was quite certain that I wasn't out of the woods yet.

I have no memory of the breathing tube coming out of my chest, but I can remember trying to croak a response to something a shovel-face had said, and being surprised that I had control over my breathing and lungs once again. I had begun to realize at that time that there were all kinds of IV lines in my arms, as well as a catheter running through me into my bladder. I wasn't happy about where I was and how I felt, but anything was better than that steel table and conveyor belt.

As time passed I was able to hold short conversations with the people that came to visit me, and take inventory of my surroundings. Even though I was out of my coma, I was still very much out of touch with reality, and while I knew I was in a hospital I had no concept of rooms or dimensions. I spent a lot of time thinking I was lying in a crib in a large round room. When doctors, nurses, or loved ones would visit me, I felt like I was looking up out of the bars of an adult sized baby crib, and they all seemed miles away from me.

Everything went by in such a blur after I came out of the coma that it is hard to describe, bits and pieces of lucidity, followed by sleep and hallucinations. My first truly lucid moment I remember is sitting up in bed and trying to eat food from a tray. My father was in a chair beside my bed urging me to eat, and I kept asking him what had happened and what was going on.

I don't remember his responses to my questions. I just remember trying to eat because dad said I needed to. I also remember feeling profoundly safe for the first time while in the hospital, because I knew my old man was there. He could be an asshole at times, but he loves his boys fiercely, and would fight the devil himself to protect any of his sons. I had no worries as long as I knew my dad was around.

I can remember seeing one of my aunts and giving her good natured hell over something or other. People that I didn't recognize would come and go from my room. At some point I realized that those cold freezing boots were not boots at all, but my own feet. What had felt to me like a month of being awake after my coma were actually only a few short days, and as soon as I was stable, the hospital began the process of moving me from ICU to a normal hospital room.

I'd had no contact with nearly anyone since I had been in the hospital, and between my mother and my friend Jenny, everyone who mattered to me was kept up to date about my progress. On my last day in ICU the transfer seemed to take forever. In a hospital, hurry up and wait is a way of life, and I seemed to be constantly watching everyone hurry-hurry-hurry to get things accomplished, only to have to then wait on someone else. I am now very glad that I had to wait to leave the ICU that day because it gave an old friend and former employee of mine the opportunity to track me down and visit with me.

Lisa Goff had known me throughout the many years I spent as the company axe-man. She had started out like most everyone, thinking I was a bad person to know. I had been in and out of her office many times over the years, and I always seemed to bring turmoil and change with me. When I had finally become the service manager of the Evansville office, Lisa had been a technician in Kentucky who worked for the Owensboro office. Shortly after I was installed in Evansville the company decided to close Lisa's office, and she was transferred to me in Evansville.

I don't know which of us was more worried about it. I knew she didn't much care for me, and Lisa has always been honest enough to make her feelings known on the subject. Well, any subject, really. Lisa has a habit of being very in your face, and she has never been afraid of expressing her opinion. She reminded me a lot of... well... me. We didn't always get along, but she had my respect, because I liked her honest, up front attitude.

That respect became mutual, and I count myself lucky to have won over this rough-cut hard-nosed woman and be able to count her as a dear friend. To anyone who ever knew me at work that thought I was nothing more than an asshole, go talk to Lisa, she will set you straight! She is honest to a fault, and she has no filter.

I think the first words out of her mouth after she walked around the corner of the door into my ICU room were "Well, you sure look like shit." Then she gave me a hug. That is Lisa, always honest even when it hurts. I really love her for that, and knowing she took the time off from work to hunt me down and visit me really bolstered my spirits. Jenny had been keeping her up to date on how I was doing in the hospital, and as soon as I was awake she had come to see me. Lisa didn't stay long, but that one simple visit did more to make me feel like myself and feel human again than anything else could have.

I am very glad I was cognizant during that visit, because for the next two weeks I would step in and out of reality often, mostly during sleep - which was often - and after the sun went down. My hurry up and wait was finally over, the transfer crew had come and was ready to take me away from the ICU and put me in a regular room on the third floor of RMC. The true extent of my illness and coma was about to be revealed to me, and my life became pure torture and pain- a living hell.

12 - VIABILITY

My new hospital room had a distinctive tropical feel, and I hated that room immensely. I don't think it was the decor that made me dislike it as much as what I would discover over the course of time that I was there. Even though I had been out of the coma, my mind was still not quite right. I hallucinated often, and everything still had a very much otherworldly feel to it.

I have been left handed all my life, and as anyone who is a lefty can attest, you take a certain pride in being different than everyone else. In grade school I always had to sit at the end of the table in the classroom, and finding a pair of scissors I could use when it was craft time was always a chore. I had always used my left hand for everything, and I was very uncoordinated with my right. So, when I discovered all of the fingers of my left hand had turned black, I was devastated. I couldn't bend my fingers, and they were nearly useless. They looked and felt as if they had been dipped in hot black plastic, then allowed to cool into stiff and distorted shapes.

My thumb and index finger were completely black to the base of the palm, and the others were nearly so. Although I wasn't supposed to, I would often find myself banging those black digits on tables, trays, and bed-rails to try and get the feeling back into them. I simply couldn't accept the fact that the fingers that had helped shape my identity on that left hand were now useless black sticks. The middle and ring finger of my right hand were also black from the tip down to the second finger-joint, but I could still feel them.

My legs were much worse off, and were a source of constant pain that I could not hide from. From my toes to several inches above my ankles had all turned black, and I could not move them. I could certainly feel them, as anything that happened to touch them, from nursing staff to a simple bed sheet caused me excruciating pain. I spent all my time on my back with my legs raised on pillows with my feet hanging off, to avoid anything touching them.

My Behcet's had taken the opportunity while I was in the coma to flare up, and I now had BD wounds all over my lower legs; My legs looked like most of the skin between knees and ankles had been peeled or carved off. This was also a major source of anguish and pain, as the wound care nurse had no idea how to care for BD skin lesions, and all her bandaging did was exacerbate the wounds.

I had finally come to the realization that the doctor that had saved my life, Dr. Kitchens, was the source of many of my coma nightmares. The first time I remember being lucid when he walked into my room I was shocked. Dr. Kitchens happens to be a dead ringer for a young Jon Cryer, and I now was facing the "Ducky" from my coma-dreams. Some part of me realized that those had all been dreams, but the part of me in control of my functions wanted nothing to do with him yet.

I was at first afraid to even look at him, much less talk to him. He had come in to discuss with my family and me what would happen next, and what might have to happen with my legs and fingers. It was then that I was told that my legs and my fingers might have to come off, and I was none too happy about it. It wasn't Dr. Kitchens call, though, and he and his team had been doing everything in their power to revive the circulation in my legs. The final call would have to come from the head of orthopedics, Dr. Donley. We were told that at the moment he was in surgery, but would call my room to set up a time to come see me and consult.

That was the very early morning, and the call came to my room before noon. The doctor would be there in an hour or so to tell me the fate of my legs. In my slightly addled state I was actually excited about the visit. I just knew that he was going to tell me that my legs would be fine, and that they wouldn't have to come off. All day we waited, and I made my parents stay with me so they could hear what the surgeon had to say. By around 7:00PM that evening the doctor hadn't shown, and we all thought I must have been mistaken about the call.

My parents finally decided to step out, thinking the doctor was a no show, and took a break to go get coffee and stretch their legs. They had been gone no time at all when the orthopedic surgeon showed up in my room more than eight hours later than promised. By this time it was late in the evening and I was none too lucid. For me the meeting was very much a haze, and the only thing I really remember about it was the unfeeling, uncaring, and rude way he told me that I had no hope. My legs weren't viable, my fingers weren't viable, and he had already set up the surgery to take my legs at the knees and all my fingers off at the palm. then he walked out.

The nursing staff found me shortly thereafter lying in my room screaming "I'm not viable! I'm not viable!" I had done my best to rip the blackened skin away from my thumb, and I was going berserk in my hospital bed. The nursing staff had to cuff me to the bed and restrain me so I wouldn't do myself any more harm. My father caught up to Donley at the nurse's station desk. He proceeded to chew that doctor's ass over going in and talking to his son while no one else was around, and told him he didn't want Donley coming near me again.

Dr. Donley, with all the arrogance he could muster, informed my father that he had no say in the matter, as my mother held power of attorney over me. When my mother was tracked down, she told him the same thing. To our amazement, Dr. Donley had not yet cancelled my surgery, and Dr. Kitchens seemed livid over the callous treatment I had received. Unfortunately for Kitchens he was only a resident, and Donley had much seniority over him, and this made it impossible for him to overrule the surgery. Kitchens informed us that, of course, if we didn't want Donley to see me again, we would have to specifically make that request. We did, and to my knowledge Dr. James Donley, that arrogant old butcher of an ortho surgeon, is no longer allowed to even *look* at my medical records.

This opened up a great many opportunities for me in the long run. The only doctor qualified to make the determination of, and perform the surgery of lower extremity amputations in the hospital was no longer allowed to see me as a patient, and Dr. Kitchens knew of a specialist in Louisville who might be able to save my limbs. If I could get well enough and strong enough to make the trip, I could be transferred.

I had a little less than two weeks to get myself strong enough to make the journey, and those two weeks would be the roughest of my life. Being fresh out of ICU and barely able to even lift my head, I had more problems than just my feet and fingers. I had only begun to start eating solid food again, and I had hardly any bodily function control. On my first day in that tropical room I missed a bedpan call three times, and I was still catheterized. After that short period of time in that third floor room I lost all shame and to this day I find it very hard to be embarrassed.

Once you have had to ask a nurse for a bedpan to go to the bathroom so many times, and then had to have the same nurse come and clean you up because you are too weak to hold yourself up, you lose all shame. I now walk around in the dead of winter wearing shorts because long pants are not as comfortable while in my prosthetic legs, and I get all kinds of strange looks from people. It doesn't bother me in the slightest - once you have had your ass wiped by a nineteen year old nurse's aide while lying in a hospital bed wearing a gown that is open in the back, you no longer get embarrassed by the little things.

My main goal in life became bodily function control and being able to remember who and where I was. Fresh off of ICU meant being constantly confused, and I would not be allowed to transfer to Louisville until I was cognizant. For the first few days on that recovery floor I called Dr. Kitchens "Dr. Joe." His first name was Joshua, but all I could catch off his name tag was the first few letters, so he was Dr. Joe. I can remember vividly him rolling his eyes at me, covering up his tag, and asking me what his name was. I couldn't remember anything more than "Joe," and so Dr. Kitchens would tell me I wasn't ready to go to Louisville yet.

During my lucid moments alone I would repeat his name to myself over and over, reading it from a scrap of paper I had asked a CNA to write his name on. I would hide that scrap of paper inside my pillow, because I was afraid that if I got caught cheating, I wouldn't get to go to Louisville. I still wasn't quite right in the head, but I learned his damned name.

I had gotten my bowel movements somewhat under control, and I was really in the mood to get the catheter out. I know I asked several times for it to be removed, but I couldn't seem to find anyone who would do it. Finally, I'd had enough and decided that I was going to remove the thing all by myself. During the coma this thing made me believe I was chained down in a store room by my crotch, so I had wanted it gone for a long, long time.

So when no one seemed to be looking, I decided to pull it out. And I did, almost. If you have never experienced a catheter, let me explain it as delicately as possible. A catheter is a thin tube that is inserted into your urethra and slowly slid all the up through your body until it reaches the bladder. Simple, really. Once there, it automatically drains your bladder into a bag, and control of your urination is not necessary. I knew all of that about catheters when I tried to pull it out. What I didn't know about was the little balloon that was inflated on the end.

That's right, at the end of the tube that is way up there in your bladder is a little balloon, and this balloon is what keeps the tube from just falling right out. I pulled that tube out a good four inches before the balloon hit rock bottom, and the small pain I had from pulling a plastic tube through my urethra was nothing compared to a balloon suddenly lodged in my bladder the wrong way. It hurt like nothing else I had ever experienced, and I made a large racket.

I had done this when my parents were gone on one of their infrequent breaks from sitting at my bedside, so when they returned they found me locked to my bed with leather cuffs. The nurses had come in to investigate my cries of pain and found my business in one hand and a catheter tube in the other, all the while me screaming in pain. The nursing staff thought I had gone crazy and tried to pull out my catheter in a fit of dementia. What had actually happened was I had tried to pull it out and caused myself a fit of pain, but it didn't matter. I had to be restrained.

I will never forget the royal dressing down I got from the nurse who had to remove that catheter after I had botched the job. The on-call doctor on the floor had to become involved, and he was none too happy about what I had done. He had to write the order for it to be removed, and then the nurse had to do it. I had to promise her I wouldn't try to pull anything else out before she would remove the tube, and then I assured her afterwards that I would use the bedside urinal she brought me.

When I finally saw the tube come out, I saw the balloon. I said, "Huh, now I know why it hurt so much and wouldn't come out." there I was, handcuffed to a hospital bed, my tender anatomy in the hands of an irritated nurse, and that was the best thing I could come up with to say. It took my parents finally returning to find their son chained to the bed to get me unshackled. By then, of course, it was getting later in the evening and the hallucinations were returning, and I was promising anyone and everyone I would be a good boy if they would just un-cuff me from the bed. Overall it was an unpleasant experience, but I did get that catheter out.

Nighttime was still the worst time for me. My parents were nearly always in my room, and all the drugs that were constantly pumped into my system gave me more strange hallucinations. I could have done myself serious damage if my folks had not been there to watch me. During the day I mainly knew where I was and why, but at night I lost all sanity and sense. I already alluded to the fact that I wasn't allowed to get out of bed to go to the bathroom, so at night I would convince myself that I must be in a hospital run by the Amish, and they didn't believe in indoor plumbing.

One night I awoke to the sound of someone urinating and the flush of a toilet. I watched through slitted eyes as my father came out the bathroom, shut out the light, and sat back down in a chair in the corner. It was late, and he went right back to sleep after his restroom visit. I was livid! I knew there had to be bathrooms in the place, and I just had my suspicions confirmed. Someone had just decided to be mean to me and not allow me the use of the toilet. Those damned Amish.

I waited until I was sure both mom and dad were fast asleep, and I worked my way to the edge of the bed. It took me forever to get the rail down, but it eventually slid down below the top of the mattress. I was so weak that I could barely sit up, so it took me quite some time to get myself sitting up, and even longer to get my legs over the side of the bed and on the floor. All I could feel of the floor was odd pressure in my knees, and I had recently had a shot of morphine so I was feeling no pain.

Just as I had worked up the resolve to try and stand up to make it to the bathroom, my mother woke up. She was at my side in an instant trying to get me back into bed, she knew I couldn't walk, but I certainly didn't at that moment. I kept telling her that I was tired of lying down in bed and peeing in a hand held urinal, and that I wanted to go pee like a man is supposed to, standing up. Mom was adamant that I wouldn't and I was just as adamant that I would.

We finally reached a compromise, mostly because my bladder was really full and I had to go, and my poor mother held the urinal for me there at the edge of the bed so I could pee like a man with my feet on the floor. When I was done she helped me get my useless legs back up onto the bed and on my prop pillows, covered me with sheets and raised my bedrail, and I went back to sleep. I look back now and realize how stupid a thing it was for me to do, but in the moment it was something I just had to do. If mom hadn't woken up I am quite certain I would have hit the floor and done myself major damage, all for wanting to go like a man.

I spent my days trying to recover enough of myself to make it to rehab, one floor up. Getting to Louisville meant being able to cope with some life basics, and the fourth floor rehab was where I could do that. All of my daytime hours were starting to clear up as long as I didn't sleep too much, and I still had a few friends coming to visit. Jenny and Bob came back, and my old friend Stephen came down with his wife Tracey and their new son CJ. I don't remember what exactly I said when I met little CJ for the first time, but Stephen stills laughs about that meeting. Hey, I was still a bit addled, and easily confused. I remember being horribly upset because Jenny and Bob were coming down and I fell asleep. Upon waking, I thought it was the next day and I had missed them. At least I figured out my mistake and confusion fairly quickly.

That became one of the scarier things for me while in that hospital, realizing that what I thought I was seeing or hearing or thinking was going on was really all in my head. I awoke one night to find the entire room was skewed to one side, and all the colors were wrong. When the television on the wall started slowly melting, I realized that it wasn't real, and the drugs were messing with my perceptions. I *knew* it wasn't real, but I couldn't do anything to make things right. The last thing I wanted to do was be alone and freaking out, so I hit the nurse call button. I asked the nurse on duty to come to my room because I was trying not to freak out, and he came right down.

I remember talking to him for a few minutes, asking him to confirm where I was and that the room wasn't really leaning, and that I was ok. He calmed me down, talked me through the haze, and kept me sane that night. When I was finally calmed down the pain was coming back in my legs, and he gave me a morphine shot that sent me blissfully to sleep. For me that was only a few minutes, I was told later by my parents that I talked to him for nearly an hour, and he told them he wouldn't leave me until I had calmed down. I can't even remember that nurse's name. I wish I could. He saved my sanity that night.

The nighttime hallucinations finally began to recede when I made it to the fourth floor, and the pain began to intensify. My legs still hurt horribly, the BD wounds on my calves were growing larger, and my feet still felt like I was wearing wet, freezing boots. The rehabilitation staff on that floor was great, but I was truly a lost cause.

I couldn't move myself around well - I was too weak from the illness and coma. Any time I moved my legs the ever-constant pain would intensify, and transferring me from bed to wheelchair was a practice in misery for all of us. I cried in pain a lot when I was on that floor, because the rehab folks were trying to get me to move my legs, to use them, but it was simply no use. I couldn't wiggle my toes, much less lay on a rehab table and do leg lifts.

The highlight of my short time on that floor was a wheel chair disguised as a recliner. When they could work me into it, I could sit reclined in relative comfort and they would wheel me out into the main hallway where I could sit and stare out a large picture window that faced the hospital parking lot. Just sitting and looking at the sun shining and the people scurrying back and forth between the parking lot and building reminded me that I was still alive. It wasn't much, but it was a start.

Unbeknownst to me, Dr. Kitchens had been relaying my progress on nearly a daily basis to the specialist in Louisville, and I was about to make the journey of a lifetime. Word finally came that I was to be transferred to Louisville's Jewish Hospital, and we once again began the process of hurry up and wait. I said goodbye to Regional Medical Center and Dr.

Kitchens' team on Halloween Day of 2010. I had been in that building for nearly five weeks, and I was glad to be moving on. I had fought long and hard to stay alive and stay sane, and while in Louisville I planned on fighting to save my legs and get out of that hospital bed and walking again soon.

13 - REALITY

The difference between Regional Medical Center and Jewish Hospital was like night and day. RMC rooms were cramped and dreary, while the rooms at Jewish were bright, airy, and roomy. There was plenty of room for my parents to find places to sleep, and the nursing staff took just as good a care of my folks as they did me.

I am very glad that most of my hallucinations were finally over, because it seems every nurse on the floor was in a Halloween costume that day. I spent the majority of my time with Jewish in the Frazier Rehab building, which was housed in nearly an entire tower of the Jewish and University of Louisville medical campus in downtown Louisville.

I had travelled by ambulance from Madisonville to Louisville, and when we finally arrived in the room it was late evening. The staff and all the colors was a balm to my psyche, and I was very glad to be somewhere I thought would make a difference. I hadn't yet met my new doctor, but I had heard plenty about him. Dr. Warren Breidenbach was an expert hand surgeon who only ten years before had completed the first double hand transplant in the United States, and he had agreed to take me on as a patient.

He was out of town when we arrived, but my

family and I had been assured that he was on a flight back to Louisville, and would be coming to meet me as soon as he landed. Several hours later we got word that he was on his way, and we patiently waited for his arrival. I was in a bit shocked when Dr. "B" breezed into the room. Of course, he had just come from the airport and wasn't dressed for work, so my first impression was slightly skewed. Dr. B is a tremendous doctor and surgeon, and has an excellent bedside manner, but my first impression was that a celebrity that I didn't recognize had just walked into my room. In all honesty Dr. B is a celebrity in the hand surgery business, and he has done some amazing work.

After introductions he took a look at my hand and legs, gave me a quick overview of his thoughts and plans for me, wished us well and breezed right back out the door. I was very glad to have finally met the specialist we had all heard so much about. Dr. B exuded confidence and knowledge from his pores, and if anyone could get me on my feet again, I was confident this was the man to do it.

I spent the next few weeks going through tests, meeting occupational and physical therapists, and a whole team of Dr. B's fellows who would be working with me. Pain was still my constant companion, and I still had ports and IV's aplenty sticking out of every available vein in my arms. Today I look like a reformed drug addict from all the scars caused by those IV jabs. The fellow doctors ran test after test, but none of them seemed very promising.

I knew I was going to lose some fingers, but my secret hope was that I would be able to keep my legs and feet. Dr. Kitchens had pulled off some miracle treatments for circulation back in Madisonville, and a good portion of my feet seemed to getting color back. Of course, with increased circulation came increased pain, and I still had all those Behcet's wounds on my lower calves. At least the wound care nurses at Jewish knew how to deal with those.

It took a nurse with nerves of steel to change those bandages, though. I can take a tremendous amount of pain, but once I have reached my limit I can and will become belligerent and ugly to whoever is causing that pain. I feel horrible about it, but I had more than one nurse leave with tears in their eyes after changing those wound bandages. I said ugly, ugly, things, and I am not proud of it. Eventually they learned to give me a pain-killing cocktail via IV before attempting to change those bandages.

I was barely a week into my stay in Louisville when Dr. B came to talk to me about my feet. So far everything they had tried to bring life back into them had failed, and we needed to discuss options. I wasn't ready to face the possibility of my legs being taken, so Dr. B offered me one final test. There was a bone scanner in the hospital, and if I could get my feet placed flat on that scanner, we could know for sure what we were looking at.

Trips down the hall and out of my room were always a chore. Well, not for me, all I had to do was take the ride in my rolling hospital bed - for everyone else it was a chore. Because I had been so sick, no one was allowed around me without a mask on, and I had to wear a paper mask anytime I was out of my room. I knew this was for my own safety, so I wouldn't become re-infected from something someone else brought into my room.

I knew it was for my own good, but it still made me feel like a pariah. Every time I was outside of the room everyone was all in masks, and anyone who saw me that was unmasked gave me a wide birth. As far as I was concerned you could have just sent a runner out ahead yelling "Outcast! Unclean! Beware! Beware!" The isolation and masks made me feel like everyone was afraid of me, made me feel like a huge bother to everyone around me.

My hurt feelings aside, a mask was what was called for on that trip to the bone scanner, so I put it on. I'm not sure exactly how it worked, but I do know I had to transfer to a cold table that raised and lowered on angles. All my hopes were pinned on that one test, if my legs were going to stay this is the test that would tell me. I was prepared for the worst as the table slowly raised my head and lowered my feet, and a large plate was raised up to touch the bottom of my feet.

When I was nearly in a full upright position I was required to put my weight on my feet, and then the scan was done. This was as close as I had come in nearly two months to standing, and instead of joy I was feeling tremendous pain. Just putting a fraction of my body weight on my feet was excruciating. I hated that test, and I never wanted to do that again. I was beginning to grow weary of the constant hurting, the always-on ache and burn, and this test hadn't helped any. I slept for hours after that test was over. The pain had finally become too much for me to handle and I was losing the fight against it.

Later that afternoon Dr. B came in to pay me a visit, and he had his entire staff of fellows with him. He and his team had reviewed the results of the scan, and the prognosis was dire. My bones from mid-calf down were dead, and there was no reviving them. I was devastated hearing this news. Dr. B kept on talking, but I didn't really hear him, I was having my own internal monologue about all the pain I had gone through thinking I would be allowed to keep my feet. I had been mentally beating myself over the head for quite some time when I realized someone was repeating my name.

I looked up to find Dr. B staring down at me with an expectant look on his face.

"I'm sorry, what?"

Dr. B repeated the statement I had earlier missed. "We can do more tests if you like. We want you to make sure of all the options before you make a decision."

Realization dawned that the doctor was telling me in the nicest way he knew that the legs needed to come off, but he wouldn't force me into a decision. He knew what needed to be done, but he wouldn't move forward until *I knew* it needed to be done. And he was giving me an out- he was giving me time to accept it if I needed to. The offer of more tests was really nothing more than an offer of more time.

More time meant more pain, and I had finally reached my breaking point over the constant pain I had been enduring since I had awoken from the coma. I looked from the doctor and his team to my parents. My mother and father had fought this fight with me every step of the way. They hadn't left my side this entire time. What I was contemplating felt like a betrayal to their sacrifice, and I had to close my eyes and look away.

My eyes were still closed when I spoke with a clear

and concise voice.

"No. No more tests. I'm tired of all this. Just take them. Take my legs."

Saying those words was -and is - the hardest thing in my life I have ever had to do. Giving up on anything is simply not my way, and having to admit that the pain and suffering had gotten the best of me meant I had failed. To the team of doctors standing around my bed it was simply a confirmation of a truth they were simply waiting for me to see: my legs were no good and they needed to go. To my parents it was a relief. They knew that we could move forward with some type of plan. To me, it was giving up and letting everyone down.

My parent had now spent a least a month out of work. When I initially went into the hospital they stayed by my side the entire time and had closed their business. They again left work behind when I transferred to Louisville, and spent the entire time with me in my room living in cramped quarters, showering in my hospital bathroom, and sleeping in fold out chairs. They had sacrificed everything for me, and by giving the go-ahead for surgery I felt like I was letting them down and flying in the face of those sacrifices they had made.

Of course the reality couldn't have been further from the truth. They wanted my pain to end just as much as I had. I have learned as a parent that when your child hurts, you hurt right along with them and my folks had hurt for me and with me every step of the way. You never know how you will react to such a life-changing decision until you have had to make it, and my reaction was shame.

I hadn't been tough enough, I had given up, and in

my own mind I was a failure. I thought my life from that point would be over, without legs I would be a freak, without legs I would be ugly, without legs I would no longer be me. It couldn't have been farther from the truth, but that is what I thought. I have peer counseled amputees before and after their surgeries, and I have heard them make the same types of comments about themselves. Telling them my story - I hope - helped them work through this *lie* every person contemplating limb loss must feel. I didn't have any peer counselors, and the only amputee peers I had in the hospital were in much worse mental shape than I was.

Once the decision had been reached, we all once again had to play the "hurry up and wait" game. My fingers would come off first, and after I had recovered from that trauma the leg surgery would be scheduled. I spent so much time simply trying to grow stronger from the illness that I can't remember what I went through between the decision and the surgery. I still couldn't lift myself into a sitting posture in bed, I still had to use a portable urinal, and I still had to call for a bedpan when I needed to have a bowel movement.

Getting me in a wheelchair was a two person operation, because I simply had no strength to help. I couldn't bathe myself, so someone had to give me baths while I lay in bed. I was so embarrassed about the shape I was in that I wouldn't let the nurse's aide come near me with a wash cloth, so my mother who had once bathed me as in infant with soap and a washcloth gave me the same bath as an adult. I was helpless, and I was getting ready to lose my fingers on my dominant hand.

When the day came for surgery all my doctors visited me, discussing what would happen, and the staff prepared me for the big move. The entire hospital complex is connected, and you can enter one building and walk through the other four or five buildings without ever stepping out into the weather. I was housed in the Frazier tower and the surgery was to be in the Jewish building.

When it was finally time to go, we all masked up and a team dedicated to patient transport took charge of my rolling bed. The team ran me all the way, and after so much time lying in one place staring at the ceiling that ride felt like a roller coaster. I did my best not to stare at my hand, but it was no use. All I could think about was my blackened fingers and the surgery I was quickly rolling towards.

My folks were allowed to come with, and once we got to the pre-surgery room they were allowed to stay until all the paperwork had been signed. If you have never had major surgery you might find it humorous to note that no matter how much you say yes, you still have to sign on the dotted line before they actually start.

After the paperwork was squared away I had one final visit from someone on my surgery team. We talked about how much they thought they could save, and what would have to go. The two fingers on my right hand still had black tips, and the doctor studied them intently. I had been given some pre surgery medications to relax me, and so I was a bit free with my words as I begged him not to take those fingertips with this surgery. I was informed they would do their best, but we would just have to see.

I actually told the doctor that if I woke up and

those right-hand fingertips were gone, "someone is going to die, because I'll kill 'em." The surgeon's fellow gave me a rather perplexed look then left the room. Hey, I was on drugs, what do you expect? I really wanted at least one complete hand, even if it was the rightie.

A nurse soon came in and started the "twilight" drugs for me, wishing me luck and asking for a countdown from ten. I don't think I got past number nine before I was out.

The further away I get from those days in the hospital the harder it is for me to remember how I truly felt about what was happening. Not long after I came home from the hospital I had started a blog, and I think the blog post written two months after I lost those precious digits might tell the tale of me meeting my new dominant hand a bit better than I can now:

"It was as big as a grapefruit, that ball of bandaging on the end of my left arm. It frightened me, that ball. I knew what was inside of it, or rather, what wasn't. I was afraid- scared shitless- of how much was not there.

See, what had been there was black. Hard, leathery, like five pieces of plastic, all pitch black and a mockery of digits. All of them my fingers. Cold on the outside and the inside. When I awoke from the delusions of coma inducing concoctions, I expected, like a fool, to be whole. Well, I was all there, but not in proper working order.

The fingers of my left hand looked like the blackened remains of a crab, mostly the legs of said crab. I could move them in a rudimentary sort of way, but they would not bend. I found the tips great for the occasional scratching of an itch, as they were so hard and pointy, but not much use for anything else.

Maybe, just maybe, under that pitch black plastic there was something still alive. We hoped, anyway. Some of that blackness peeled away, revealing tortured, but pink, flesh. Living flesh. But not enough. Thus the frightening ball of bandages.

What was under there? What was not? I felt like I still had fingers, but knew the deranged nervous system and its tortured nerve endings would lie, giving me false hope. Telling tales that were pure flights of fancy.

I held off having the bandages removed until the nurse practically forced me. When they unwrapped that ball, I held my eyes tightly shut. I didn't want to see. Morbid curiosity finally pried my eyes open, and then those eyes flooded. I don't remember for certain, but I think a wail accompanied that flood of tears.

The mangled remains of my hand, my good hand, my dominate hand, was more than I could handle.

Gone was my thumb. Gone was my index finger. The rest, well, they were ugly, to say the least. Swollen and bulbous stumps, black stitching everywhere, my hand was a ruin of flesh. The one and only consolation given was that there was no pain. Of course, my hand never hurt to begin with.

The tips of my middle and ring finger on my right hand were black as well. Those were to go as well. I begged and pleaded with the hand surgeon's subordinate fellows not to take those tips. I knew there was good flesh under there. I could feel it. They listened, and at least my right hand is whole."

I hadn't held my dad's hand since I was a little boy, but when I saw that wreck of a hand I cried like a baby at what I saw. Then my dad was there by the side of the bed and he took my good right hand in his own and he told me it was going to be ok. I had spent the better part of my life trying to be strong and tough, to be like the man my father was, and there he was sitting by my bed holding my hand. There were unshed tears in his eyes, and in thirty seven years that was the first time I had ever seen my father come close to crying. My dad held my hand until I finally cried myself to sleep. That was the end of the first week of November, 2010, slightly over two short months since I had first been admitted into the emergency room at Madisonville.

I had pulled through the surgery without a hitch, and I was informed that my leg surgery had been scheduled for the following week. I spent most of that time trying to learn to feed myself again and starting occupational and physical therapy for my hand. The hospital food was horrible, and bending what was left of my fingers and hand was no fun. Funny, I can't remember much about that time in between surgeries *except* that the food was so bad. The doctors would gripe at me for not eating enough, and I would gripe about how bad the food tasted.

All that time really was for me was a countdown, a hurry up and wait for the surgeries that would take my legs away. We were all hoping for the best because of how well the finger surgeries had gone, getting to keep more of my fingers and hand than what the surgeon in Madisonville had planned. In my first meeting with Dr. B after the hand surgery he told us that he thought I would be able to keep part of my legs below the knees. He also asked me about my reaction and tears after seeing my hand for the first time.

"I hear from my nurse you were unhappy with my

work," was all he said on the subject. To this day I don't know if he was being serious or trying to be funny. He did do excellent work. You can't see any of the suture scars on my hand at all.

I had some of the OT and PT staff talk to me a bit about prosthetics, but I wasn't ready to think about my legs being gone, much less fake legs. I spent a lot of time that week looking at my legs and feet, trying to remember everything about them because they would soon be gone. The skin of my feet and lower calves had darkened, and I could feel nothing but constant, intense pain from them. The entirety of my lower legs was covered in bandages with long strips of skin completely eaten away by the Behcet's. What was left of my legs wasn't pretty, but I just couldn't stop looking.

The day of my leg amputations finally came, and I was nervous and scared, as well as a bit excited. I was still feeling like I had let everyone down with the decision to take my legs, but the thought of no more pain made me excited. I felt guilty about it, but I was looking forward to being pain-free.

Surgery time came and went, but we had been warned that things might go behind schedule. When the transport team finally came we once again masked up and I was given Mr. Toad's Wild Ride down to the same surgery center I had been in the week before. Like a carbon copy of my previous operation there was paperwork, explanations, and pre-surgery visits. Dr. B came in for this one, and I was asked a question that I will never forget. Did I want my legs to be sent home for burial, or would I like them incinerated?

My answer was short and concise. "Burn them." Those things had turned my world into nothing but pain, and knowing that there would be nothing left but ashes just felt right to me. And besides, we have all seen the "Evil Dead" movies, right?

This time around I wasn't put out until I reached the surgery room, and the short glimpse I got of that room still haunts me. Too-bright lights and oddities hanging from the ceiling, with rolling trays all around. There were nurses scurrying about in preparation for things to come, and I was grateful when the anesthesiologist came and asked me to count back from ten. I didn't count this time. I was about to have major life-changing surgery performed, I was about to lose my legs. Counting just wouldn't do, because I knew there was a possibility something might go wrong and I might not wake up. I said the one thing I have always relied upon when I have been truly afraid, the thing that kept me strong when all else failed.

Hail Mary, full of grace. The Lord is with thee..........

And then the syringe's plunger dropped and the lights went out.

14 - STRONGER

It turned out I nearly didn't wake up from that surgery at all, and after it was over I spent a few short days in another coma, in another ICU room. Something happened that made my vitals drop as things were coming to a finish, and they nearly lost me on the table. My parents couldn't stay in the ICU room with me, so they were sent away to worry and wonder in a hotel room.

When I finally awoke, the first thing I was asked to do was take a drink of water. It seems the abilities to both swallow and urinate are rather important after surgery and anesthesia, and I goofed up the swallowing bit. In my defense, I wasn't even yet fully awake when the cup was pressed into my hand, and the water went down the wrong way and I choked a bit. That one little incident would make my next few weeks a living hell, and cause me to have a true hatred for the specialist who handed me that cup. Because I had one episode of choking, she decided that I would not be allowed any true liquids, and a feeding tube was inserted through my nose and down into my stomach. I was miserable.

Every liquid that came my way had a thickener put into it, and all the water I drank had to be sucked through a tiny sponge on the end of a lollipop stick. I was constantly thirsty, and I simply was not allowed to take a normal drink. Because the food was so bad I really wasn't eating that much, and my folks spent a lot of time ordering in food for me, or going out to pick up fast food.

I have been a coffee drinker since my teenage years, and a nice hot cup of java in the mornings is a must for me. Under orders, my coffee would come on my breakfast tray with thickener added, making it the consistency of runny jello or honey. I don't know if you have ever tried eating your morning cup o' joe with a spoon, but I have. I don't recommend it. The feeding tube sent a constant stream of sludge into my stomach with all the nutrients a growing boy needed, and as soon as it hit my small intestines that sludge turned to concrete.

So there I was eating my coffee and using my intestines as a concrete mold, trying not to look at what was left of my legs. It was so very odd to look at the severed endings to my legs just a few short inches from my kneecaps. My pain was different, not a whole lot less, but different. It was more tolerable, and I was no longer in a constant agony. I kept repeating to myself *I can't believe my legs are gone - I can't believe my legs are gone....*

I was in mental shock. I had been preparing myself for this inevitability for so long and yet I was still having trouble accepting the fact that I no longer had calves or feet. I wasn't allowed to sit alone and think about it very much, though, because I had just been introduced to my new nemesis, a physical therapist named Mike. Mike was a real slave driver, and I give him and his fellow PT Emily much of the credit for my initial recovery. Mike and Emily worked me to the bone and never allowed me to slack. The very first day he walked into my room he brought a team with him to get me into a wheelchair and roll down to the therapy room. One of my first questions for him was, "What if I don't want to go?" His response was simple yet profound. I didn't have to go if I didn't want to, but if I didn't go to therapy what was the point of me being there?

Between that and a young lady I had met briefly in the hall outside of the therapy room doors, I made my decision to do everything I could to fight back and get better. I don't know the young lady's name or her story; I just know that I didn't want to be like her. She was one of the few amputees I would meet during my time at Frazier rehab, and she was sitting in a wheelchair in front of the nurse's station quietly staring down at her one amputated leg. She had lost her right leg below the knee, and wrapped around the end was a high tech carbon fiber prosthetic leg.

That prosthesis was the first I had ever seen close up, and I knew then and there I needed to work hard, because I wanted some of those! Shiny and black, reminiscent of something in a sci-fi movie on a cyborg, or what might be hidden under the flesh of a Terminator. I never got to say a word to this young lady, but I would often get to hear her during therapy sessions. She cried all the time, fought with her therapists, and I dubbed her the "Crybaby."

Those first few days in that state-of-the-art therapy room I would be laid onto a therapy platform and introduced to wedges, blocks, and other assorted shapes all done up in foam rubber. Sitting up, laying down, or on my side those shapes would be wedged against me so I could lift my legs, bend my knees, raise my arms, and try to bring some semblance of strength back to my weakened body. While I would lay on that padded table quietly crying, tears rolling from my eyes from the pain of moving my tortured limbs, Crybaby would sit in her wheelchair and scream at the PTA's who were trying to get her up and moving.

I began to dread hearing her cries, and every time she screamed, "NO! NO! I don't want to!" I would steel myself against my pain and work all the harder, but my pain seemed to be getting worse. I assumed this was normal, I had just had my legs amputated below the knees, so obviously some things were going to hurt, and I spent several days working out on that table with my silent tears before one of my therapists caught me at it.

The pain that they made me describe was much more than would be expected, and one of my surgeons was called in to take a look. The distal ends of my legs ("distal end" is the anatomical term for the end of an amputated limb, I refuse to ever use the term "stump," as I find it offensive) were always wrapped up in long ace bandages, and wrapping them up is somewhat of an art. The doctor who came in to look at my right leg - which had been causing me all the pain - had barely gotten the wrappings off before the look of concern crossed his face.

I was rushed off for some sort of scan, and it was determined that a hematoma had developed at the end of my right leg. All therapy was stopped, and an emergency surgery was scheduled and then performed. My distal ends were already short due to the Behcet's leaving so little good skin left to use, and now my right leg would lose more bone, and become even shorter than the left.

This didn't make much of a difference to me, as my legs were already gone and all I wanted was the hematoma pain to go away. My mom and dad were still constantly by my side. Off we went again for a ride to surgery, and I had to start the recovery process all over again.

Recovery was harder for me this time around, as my doctors soon realized that my blood pressure was beginning to once again drop, and they had no idea why. After much testing, an echocardiogram revealed a problem with my heart. Not only had I lost my legs and fingers due to the sepsis, now it seemed I had a hole in my heart that was constantly leaking blood. I was still eating coffee in the mornings and enjoying sips of water through a sponge, and I could now enjoy listening to the pros and cons of cracking open my chest for heart surgery while I spooned my java-jello.

I count myself very lucky that the Jewish hospital system is staffed with a multitude of specialists because I had one heart surgeon wanting to crack open my chest, and another that didn't think I needed it. My heart would heal itself with time, that second doctor said, and surgery wasn't required. That doctor would be found right over time, and I was spared having to add open heart surgery to my growing list of procedures.

My parents and I had an angel of sorts come to us during the time right after that second surgery, although I don't think even his wife would call him "angel." My old boss Damon lived in Louisville, and he stopped by the hospital to pay me a visit. Without Damon's efforts my recovery would not have been nearly as good as it had been, as he made sure that my letter of resignation was never processed and that I was instead put through the company system of sick pay and then short term disability. This allowed me to still have somewhat of an income, as well as being able to keep my insurance benefits.

My parents had been continually living in my hospital room with me, living off of cafeteria food and grabbing showers in my hospital room as they could. It didn't take long into that visit from my old boss to see that my folks needed a break from the hospital and from all that was happening. He offered to take care of a hotel room for them for a week or two so they could have a break. Damon's thoughtful gift gave my parents some much needed alone time, a chance to decompress, as well as the opportunity to sleep in a real bed again.

Throughout the years Damon Bayens had always come through for me at work, keeping me on-point, pushing me to better myself, and teaching me how to do the job the right way regardless of consequences. To some, his gift may seem like a small thing but to me it was - and is - tremendous. He gave my parents a much needed break when they needed it the most, and I can never thank him enough for all he has done.

After both the hematoma and heart issue was dealt with, I dove back into therapy with one goal in mind: recovery. One of the first things I had to do was learn to get into a wheelchair without help, and the tool of choice for the job is called a slide board. A slide board is either a plastic or wooden plank not much bigger than a skateboard platform, and it is used to literally slide from bed to chair, and back again.

When you lose twenty or more pounds from the

lower portion of your body, your center of gravity shifts. Sitting up on my own was hard enough because I was still so weak, and now I had to learn to sit on the edge of a bed without falling off. I mastered that in no time, but the slide board was another thing entirely. The first time I transferred from bed to wheelchair there were two therapists on hand to coach me, and I was scared to death.

When you have no feet the floor looks miles away, and your greatest fear is falling. I might as well have been walking a tightrope across the Grand Canyon, as the floor was so far away and I had nothing but a slick piece of wood between me and the total destruction of hitting that floor. I squealed like a frightened schoolgirl when I slid my cheeks over that vast expanse between the bed and the chair, and when I made it I did nothing but close my eyes and shake.

Wheelchairs were uncomfortable, because I was forced to let my distal ends hang, and that made them swell and ache. I have to give Mike credit. I put the poor guy through hell trying to find the perfect amount of support for the ends of my legs. Custom wheelchair supports, blocks of foam rubber, rolled up towels, and wheelchair calf supports were all tried, but to no avail. Nothing seemed to work, and all those things did was make the ache worse. Mike finally came up with the simplest thing in the world, and I soon found myself rolling around with two strategically placed hospital pillows under my distal ends.

I had somewhat mastered the art of the slide board and I could now sit in a wheelchair without total misery, so Mike decided it was high time I started pushing myself around. With only one good hand this was a chore, as I tended to push myself in circles, but he had a fix for that. Rubber tubing was added on the left side wheel rail, and I could now get a bit of grip with what was left of my hand. To this day if I happen to be in a wheelchair I still tend to list to the left a bit as I roll, but I rarely run into anything anymore. Well, most of the time, anyway.

Now that I was rolling and getting back to the therapy gym, the tube in my nose and the lollipop sponge had to go. If you complain about anything enough, you will eventually get your way. And I complained a lot about that damn tube. The sludge that had been constantly pumped into my system had slowed my bowel movements to a stop, and I had had enough. I was still forced to use the call button to ask for bedpans, and I hadn't been to sit in a normal bathroom since September.

A nurse even had to strategically place a suppository to allow me to have a bowel movement, and I now know what it feels like to give birth. I began telling every nurse and doctor that came into my room that they had a deadline, if they didn't remove that tube and let me drink like a normal person I was going to pull the tube out myself. I generally had a good reputation as a patient, and I always made it a point to thank the nursing staff after they gave me treatments, changed bandages, or gave me medications.

If you ever happen to find yourself in an extended hospital stay, keep in mind that the staff there is paid to keep you alive and get you better, not put up with yelling and screaming from the patient. Some of the bandage changes I had to endure were lengthy and extremely painful, and no matter how much it hurt, I made sure I always thanked the nurse or aide before they left. Oh, I know I said a few ugly things when the pain was too much, and I made more than one nurse cry, but I always apologized, and I always thanked them. *Don't be an asshole to the people who control your pain meds* is a good rule of thumb in any hospital setting.

I had reached the point of no return with that feeding tube, though. The final time I had to mention to a nurse that I was going to pull it out if they didn't, she giggled at me and said, "you know if you get it out we will just put it right back in!" Just for a moment I became a true asshole as I grabbed the tube and began removing the tape that held it too my face.

"If I pull this out on my own I would God-Damned like to see any of you try and put it back in. I *will* hurt someone. Now get that doctor that ordered this fucking tube and tell her I'm taking it out today if she doesn't!"

I don't even feel all that bad about saying it, I was so tired of the tube and the water sponge. It took perhaps twenty minutes to get the specialist in the room, and apparently the nurse told her I meant business. I was immediately sent down for a live x-ray of my esophagus, and I got that damned tube taken out. The test was simple; I had to eat food laced with barium in front of an x-ray camera. It was actually pretty cool to watch the television screen and see the food get chewed and then swallowed. I passed that test, and the tube was removed as soon as I got back to my room. I did apologize to the nurse for having to be rude, and she told me not to worry about it. She repaid me for my transgressions the very next day. She volunteered to be the nurse who removed the stitches from my fingers. There were a lot of them, and it hurt. I deserved it, though.

Occupational Therapy began to play a larger role in my time at Frazier Rehab, and I was very glad of it. Bedpans were getting old, and I wanted to begin having a somewhat more normal existence. I was still very weak, and had trouble moving around in a hospital bed without feet. One might be surprised at how difficult it is to move around on a bed without having feet or heels. It takes practice.

One of my very early attempts at going to the bathroom without help involved a bedside toilet chair and me backing out onto it from the bed. Since I couldn't yet make it to the bathroom on my own, and I was still terrified of slide board transfers, the suggestion was made that the commode could be pushed directly up against the bed and I could slide from the bed directly onto the commode. My mother pushed it into place for me and held it, and I slowly backed myself out onto the seat.

Of course, once I got there, I couldn't go, and I soon discovered I couldn't push myself back onto the bed. After much squirming and moving, I was finally able to get myself onto the bed, but I was now on my belly and my head was at the foot of the bed! I had totally worn myself out just getting back into bed and yet I refused any help from my mother to get me back in the proper position in the bed.

I was so weak that I was laying on one of my arms and couldn't get it out from underneath me. I worked and worked and worked just to finally get it pulled out, but I was still stuck wrong-way-round, belly-down on the bed. I had been at it for about half an hour when one of my OT's came in to get me for a therapy session. My mother quickly explained what had happened, and informed her I was being stubborn and refusing any help to get back in the right position.

I spent nearly the next half hour working my way up to the top of the bed and rolling over. The occupational therapist would offer suggestions but would not touch me, honoring my stubborn request to do this on my own. When I had myself turned around and once again on my back, I felt like I had finally won a small victory. Rolling from your belly to your back then turning around in bed is nothing- try it yourself sometime. It took everything I had and an hour's time to complete the task, but I had done it on my own. I had had my first victory, the first of many fights I would take on and win. I still had to go to the bathroom, though.

I grew stronger day by day after that. I was healing, the infection was gone, the hole in my heart had healed, and I was learning to be human once again. I had finally learned how to transfer from a chair to a toilet, and for the first time in months I could flush when I was done, as opposed to hitting a call button and asking for a bedpan removal. I learned to brush my teeth again, I learned how to shower on my own, and I could even put my own clothes on and dress myself again.

The staff of Frazier worked me very hard, and I can never thank them enough for all the challenges that they gave me. Without my time there I would be nothing more than a lump in a wheelchair. Dr. Williamson, who was the head of rehabilitation, made the decision that they had done all they could for me for the time being, and it was time for me to return to Madisonville to finish out my physical therapy.

Everyone was excited about getting back home. My parents had now spent more than two months by my side and away from work, and they were ready to get me home so life could get back to normal. It was the first week of December, 2010, and the day dawned bright and beautiful as we prepared for the afternoon ambulance trip that would bring me one step closer to home. Mike, my PT, came in that morning and told me about this prosthetic guy who did excellent work that he wanted me to meet before I left, and with my ok he called and set up a time for this leg guy to come talk to me.

Up until that point the thought of prosthetics for me was mostly abstract, some future goal for some future time. The thought of actually walking again was like watching a foreign film. It was a pretty picture to look at, but even with subtitles I still didn't really get it. I had worked so hard just to learn to go to the bathroom by myself. I was a long way from prosthetic legs, right?

When I met Matt Hayden from Kentucky Prosthetics for the first time I didn't know what to think of him. I was expecting someone dressed like a doctor, who would speak in technical terms and tell me maybe I might walk again sometime in the future. He was dressed nothing like a doctor in his Nike golf shirt and khaki pants, and talked nothing like a doctor. If anything he reminded me very much of Mike, down to earth and plain speaking.

As a new amputee I was very sensitive about anyone looking at or touching my residual limbs (another term for distal ends that doesn't bring to mind chopped down trees) and I was leery of this quick exam from a perfect stranger. After looking my legs over Matt asked me about what I had done in my life, and what I had enjoyed doing before I became ill.

I talked about fighting fires and rappelling, motorcycle riding and Jiu Jitsu, and hanging out with my son. Matt told me that I could do all of those things again, and he could help me do it. I might have to ride a trike instead of a two-wheeler, but otherwise he thought he could get me back to doing 98% of the things I had done before limb loss. He also informed me he could have me in a pair of legs again in months, not the years that I expected.

Matt told me to talk to a few more prosthetics places if I wanted to make sure I found the best fit for my needs and goals, but I was already sold. I wanted no one else to make my legs, this man promised to get me back to ninety-eight percent, and I wasn't letting go of that promise. Matt gave me a bag with helpful information for new amputees, his card, and some funny looking socks called "shrinkers." I would grow to have a love/hate relationship with those shrinkers - as they hurt like hell on my distal ends, but I put them on because Matt said I needed to. When he walked out of my room that day I had hope for the first time in a long time. I had hope of a normal life. I would be strong again, I would walk again, and Matt Hayden was going to help me get there.

15 -ALMOST HOME

When I left Regional Medical Center nearly five weeks prior, I was a pitiful lump of a human being with blackened fingers and legs and nothing but pain on my mind. When I returned I was a triple amputee learning how to be human once more with the singular goal of getting better and walking again.

I landed on the physical therapy floor of the hospital with a plan for two weeks of both physical and occupational therapy. I was somewhat of an oddity on that floor, as bilateral lower extremity and upper extremity amputation on one individual is rather uncommon in the amputee community. You tend to see multiple upper and lower limb loss patients in the media, but that is simply because those stories are all the more heart wrenching, and get better viewership and ratings. The average amputee has a single limb loss and the usual suspect for the cause is diabetes in those of a more mature age. You simply don't hear about those amputees as often because diabetes doesn't sell. Traumatic accidents, wounded warriors, and automotive wrecks do. Regardless of how the amputations occurred, the result for most all amputees is the same - a lot of hard work.

Hard work was the order of the day for me on the PT floor of RMC. I was lucky enough to know some of the people that worked with me, and those familiar faces helped me remember what it was to be - and act - like a normal person. Strict routines are set during therapy, and just like at Frazier I had a daily regimen of meals, workouts, and therapy.

I learned to hate a small machine that looks like bicycle pedals on a stand, and I spent a lot of time pedaling to nowhere with my arms and hands. I spent more time on therapy tables honing my new balance and mastering this strange new center of gravity I had, and doing countless leg lifts to help my now-atrophied thigh muscles. I had spent a lifetime walking miles and miles every day at work, as well as crawling in the cramped confines under the substructure of homes and buildings. Coupling that with all my accumulated mat time with wrestling and Jiu Jitsu over the years had given me thighs and calves as thick and solid as tree trunks.

My calves were now gone, and the muscles in my thighs were now like jello. All that time lying in a hospital bed had turned my strong legs into nothing more than flab. Toned and well defined musculature was now nothing more than a soft and rounded mass of pasty flesh. My upper body hadn't fared quite as badly, as I had begun to rely on my shoulders, arms, back, and chest to move me around the bed and facilitate transfers to and from wheelchairs. Overall I was thin to the point of wasting away from all that I had been through, but not my poor legs.

So every day my therapy team worked my legs hard. Since I had not walked in nearly three months and had multiple surgeries close to them, my knees were stiff and unyielding. I continued a regimen of knee bend exercises started by Mike at Frazier, and every day I would lay a tightly rolled pillow made of hospital towels and tape under my knees and work toward bending and flexing my knee joints. It would take months to get my full range of motion back in my left knee and while my right has never completely returned I have at least 95% movement in it. I still have that rolled-up towel-pillow Mike made stuck away in a drawer somewhere.

I had spent plenty of time at Frazier learning all the basics of living in a wheelchair with their Occupational Therapy staff, so for me, OT at Madisonville wasn't as much of a priority. I knew how to transfer myself from bed to chair to bathroom, and I had mastered the art of dressing myself while lying in a hospital bed. I could bathe myself with the use of a shower chair, and I could brush my own hair and teeth. These are all things that most take for granted every day, but for someone without lower limbs and stuck in a wheelchair all of those things can be a challenge.

Bathing was the hardest thing simply because it wore me out. I had to first make it to the bathroom, then undress in the wheelchair, then take my slide-board and make my way out onto the shower chair over the tub. Shower chairs are a scary thing for me, sitting naked on a large slab of plastic while you're wet and soapy is a recipe for disaster - especially when you can't put your feet down to steady yourself. I haven't used a shower chair since I first came home from the hospital, I just don't trust the things.

After you're done cleaning yourself you have to dry off, get back into your wheelchair and then dress yourself in clean clothes while sitting down. The entire process would take me more than an hour, and by the time I was done I was ready for a nap.

Going to the bathroom while at RMC was always a chore, as I had one particular nurse who seemed to think I could not go in by myself. At the time I had to use a bedside commode over the top of the regular toilet, as the wider seat and side-handles gave me a more confident grip. Every time my bathroom-guard was on shift she would berate me if she caught me going in by myself, and every time I would argue and fight with her. I simply refused to use the toilet with a large female nurse standing over me. Not gonna happen.

We finally reached a compromise after I had cursed at her enough, and she would stand outside the door and listen. When I got down to business the bathroom would become quiet, and when the silence lasted too long I would hear a *tap-tap-tap* on the door and the nurse asking "How are things going in there?" Things wouldn't "go" anywhere in there while she was talking, and knowing she was hovering just outside the door during bathroom sessions when she was on shift was tedious. As soon as she would hear the flush she would try to open the door to help me get my pants back on, this woman just wouldn't quit! I always staved off her advances, and I know she meant well, but she made bathroom time no fun.

Bathroom time is no fun to begin with when you have to use a wheelchair. If you ever want to know what a wheelchair bound amputee has to do just to use the restroom, feel free to pull out any hard-seated chair in your house and have a seat. Pick and keep your feet up off the floor a bit and then take off your pants, when your done with that just put them back on, all while remaining seated and your feet off the floor. It's fun, go try it. Really.

Being on a therapy floor in a small hospital, I was the only amputee and the youngest person there. Most of my fellow patients were elderly and recovering from strokes, broken hips or bones, or major surgery. Most of us were in wheelchairs and it was a sobering thought for me to realize even with my amputations I was the only person there with a long-term possibility of not staying in that prison-on-wheels. We all got together during meals to eat, talk, and socialize, telling each other about our therapies, our progress, our lives, and our children. I was the only person there with a child still in school, and the only person who didn't have grandkids.

Being on that floor also meant that I was much closer to home, and I no longer had to have my parents as room-mates. I was well enough and close enough that mom and dad could be at home again and could finally return to work. They would come to visit me in the evenings then go home. My son's mother lived in Madisonville, and throughout my entire ordeal she had made sure that my boy was at my side as often as possible.

I hadn't had many visitors while in Louisville, so being closer to home meant my friends could make it in to see me. My buddy Bob is a car and motorcycle guy, and he relates a lot of things in life to those two things. From the first moment I met him he has called me "One-wheel-peel-Neil" and I was never so glad to hear that irritating homage to limited-slip differentials and my name as when they came to visit.

The last time I'd really had visitors I was fresh out of a coma and everything seemed like a three-ring psycho-circus. Now I was fully cognizant, in much less pain, and able to really enjoy their visits. My older brother Kyle got to stop by once or twice, and my younger brother Wes came up several nights just to watch television with me. The TV show *The Walking Dead* had just premiered, and I was instantly hooked. We both have always loved the zombie apocalypse genre, so watching that sitting in my hospital room after dinner really made me feel like my old self again. It was such a simple and normal thing watching TV with my little brother, shooting quick quips at each other about the show, laughing at the things only we could think were funny. It was normal, and it made me feel a little bit normal again.

I had made so much great progress in my therapy between Frazier and RMC, it was decided that my two week stay would be shortened to only about eight days, and on December 15th, 2010, I was released from the hospital, able to go home for the first time in nearly three months. My folks had a nice big comfortable truck, but unfortunately it was much too tall for me to attempt to get into. My father borrowed a low-slung car from a friend of the family, and for the first time since my illness I rode in a car.

Getting in that rear seat was a chore in and of itself for me. I had mastered simple slide-board transfers, but the gap and height distance between that car seat and my wheelchair seemed huge. Jonathan, one of the PTA's that had worked with me during my stay followed us out, and promised that he wouldn't let me fall. I practically had to drag myself across that huge twelve inch expanse between my chair and the car, and the winter-cold concrete beneath me looked miles and miles away.

Jonathan got me in the car without once hitting the ground, and we headed home. This was my first time riding in a vehicle without feet to put on the floorboards, and every little turn and slow-down threw me everywhere. When you don't have feet on the floor, every stop throws you forward as if the brakes were slammed, and needless to say the entire ride was an experience. I had been stuck in a hospital for what seemed like forever, and this was the first time in months I got to watch the landscape slide by outside a car window, and that landscape was starting to look very much like home.

When we pulled into my parents' driveway I was nervous, I had spent so much time with tubes, needles, IV's, and monitors either stuck in me or stuck on me that I felt odd and somewhat naked without them. I was seeing an entire world I had once known from the new perspective of a wheelchair, and everything looked a bit foreign. The first thing I noticed as we pulled under the carport was a long wooden ramp that had been built against the side of the house leading to the porch. I was a member of the local Veterans of Foreign War Men's Auxiliary, and they had decided to pay for - and then install - a ramp for me.

Getting out of the car and into the wheelchair was easier than getting in, and my father turned me around and headed up the ramp. I had been practically carried out of this house when all this started, and here I was sitting in front of the door of my childhood home without legs or fingers, in a wheelchair. Dad got the door unlocked and then asked me if I was ready. I nodded, and he rolled me into the house, and into my new life as an amputee.

PART THREE

16 - HOME SWEET HOME

My place in Bowling Green had been small, but I really enjoyed it. It was an apartment styled more like a condo than your average apartments stacked one on top of the other, and both doors opened directly to the outside. The rear door opened out onto a small patio and I had spent many evenings after work sitting out on that tiny slab of concrete reading. I had my own detached garage where I spent my weekends modifying my Suzuki when I wasn't out riding it. I haven't even seen my building since my mother drove me away from it when I first got sick.

Everyone had been told I was going to die, so my family did their best to get all of my affairs in order. My mother was granted power of attorney to handle my finances and bills, and my brother Kyle and his wife Kim went down to my little place to clean it out. My mother's sister Phyllis and my cousin Lisa and her husband met Kyle and Kim there to help. In a weekend, they took everything I had and either packed it away in storage or pitched it, getting that apartment ready to go back to the property manager. I still don't know where all my stuff is, and I have been assured that most of it is still in storage, *somewhere*.

Most of my clothes were washed and put away, my

furniture was kept, and my tools and motorcycle found a new home in a small and empty house my folks own next door to their own home. My truck went to live at Kyle's place in Nashville for a while, and my entire existence in South Central Kentucky was obliterated from the map. I know of a few things that were pitched, and the one that hurts the most was a workout bag that had my nicely worn and faded Jiu Jitsu Gi and the third level orange belt I had earned from my Jiu Jitsu instructor, Eric Myers. I can't blame any of them for pitching what they did, as far as they were concerned they were cleaning out the house of a family member who had for all intents and purposes *died*.

I had no property. I had no home. Coming to my parents' place after the hospital was my only option, and honestly it was my best option. I was not ready to take care of myself, and I was going to need a lot of help and support to get better. My parents had raised three sons to adulthood and helped me raise my own son, and we had all gone out into the world and made our own homes. They had finally gotten a well-deserved break from raising kids, and had achieved their empty nest. Now they were bringing home a son to care for in a way they never expected.

In some ways I was no different than a toddler, except I couldn't toddle. I had mastered the art of feeding myself and going to the bathroom, but I was still weak. The simplest things tired me out, and I was miserable most of the time because I was still coming to terms with what had happened to me. I was a thirty-seven year old man who lived with his parents, and I still couldn't believe I had lost my legs.

Mom and Dad had worked very hard to make the

house as comfortable as possible for me. My boyhood room was upstairs and those stairs were completely out of the question for me, so my new bedroom became the smallest room on the ground floor. I had spent a lot of time in that room when I was younger because it housed the first computer I had ever had a chance to play with. My new bedroom was the old office.

A full sized bed with a thick topper took up most of the room, and that bed was taller than the armrest of my wheelchair. Transferring from chair to bed was like climbing a mountain, and the transfer back felt like a playground slide, a really scary, steep playground slide. I had just enough room to get my chair in between the closet and the bed, and maneuvering could be a chore in my room. That first day home was a tough one for me, and after I finally got up into that big bed I spent most of my time crying silent tears. My life had been reduced to a big bed in a tiny room.

There was a stand-alone bathroom across the house in the laundry room that my parents completely gutted and then made wheelchair accessible for me. The shower now had a fancy slide-chair for getting in and out of, and the gorgeous sink and cabinet had been replaced with an open and industrial looking bathroom sink, much like in the hospitals. They even replaced the door to make sure I had enough room to get in. A disabled-accessible toilet chair had been placed over top of the commode with sliding hand rails on each side.

I was so thankful that they had done that for me, but I hated it. It was such a reminder- now that I was home-that I was handicapped, that I was no longer *normal.* In the hospital, being handicapped was sort of an abstract idea for me. I was being taught and trained how to live this new life, but I was in a hospital where things like that are the norm. Now that I was home it was staring me in the face. *I'm a freak, I live with my parents, my life is over...*

My being home meant life could go on for everyone else, and I quickly had to acclimatize myself to being truly alone for the first time in months. Both of my parents returned to work, and although they worked less than three minutes away they were still gone. I no longer had nurses coming in to take my blood pressure or listen to my heart, my bed had no call button, and I no longer heard the quiet hums and buzzes that can only be found in a hospital room. The silence I experienced when I was alone in the house was eerie.

There was a flat-screen in the room on top of a dresser, but I couldn't make use of it as it wasn't connected to the satellite dish service. I found myself spending most of my time sitting on that bed with my legs propped up, my laptop computer lying on my belly. I did my best to read, post, and respond on my social media sites, and keep up with friends. My television watching had been reduced to what I could stream to that tiny screen, and boredom was a constant companion.

Gaming on the computer was out of the question, as with only one usable hand I couldn't use the keyboard effectively, and my one saving grace with the computer was that nearly everyone in the house except my father was right handed when we first started using computers, so he and I both had learned to use a mouse with our right hands. I would get nearly hourly calls from my mom that first week that I was home and she and dad were at work, so I at least had human contact.

My friends would call as well, and that helped me a lot. You never know how many true friends you really have until you nearly die and lose some limbs. I had friends and I was glad of them, as they really kept me connected, rooted, and sane. I had a lot of friends come visit those first few months I was home, and I cherished every visit. Jenny and Bob would make the trip down from Evansville nearly every other weekend. My good friend Matthew Williams made the trip down from Lexington to see me, and I even had an old high school buddy we all called Poo-Bah make a visit.

I would do my best to look happy and well, and we would sit at the kitchen table and talk about anything and everything. I always felt a bit awkward sitting there in my prison-on-wheels with the ends of my legs barely making it over the edge of the seat, and my ruined hand usually covered by my good hand because I was ashamed of the way it looked. They all tried to pound it into my head that although my body looked different I was still me on the inside. That was a tough thing for me to comprehend at the time because my outside has always been what I saw in the mirror, and always how I defined myself. I think every amputee goes through this in the beginning, thinking they are a different person because their body is now different, but it simply isn't true. What you look like on the outside *does not* define who you are on the inside, and you should never let *anyone* tell you differently.

I was home slightly less than two weeks when

Christmas rolled around, and my entire family had something joyous to celebrate that year, namely me. I had talked enough about my problems with trying to use my laptop that word had spread to my brothers, and I was surprised on Christmas morning with some truly excellent gifts. Kyle and Kim had gotten me an iPad, and my brother Wes and my folks had gotten me all sorts of accessories to go with it.

That gift truly opened up a new world for me. I now had a small device that could sit in my lap that I didn't need a keyboard or mouse to operate. I could type fairly quickly one-handed, and I soon learned that what was left of my pinkie on my left hand could be used for tapping and typing on the on-screen keyboard. Suddenly I could game again, as touch screen controls could be configured however I wanted them, and the small size was easy to deal with.

The game I played the most when I first got that tablet was of all things *Angry Birds*. If you have never seen it, it is nothing more than a silly little game where you sling-shot chubby little birds at pigs hiding in fortresses, and your goal is to pop all the little piggies. It is a fun little time-burner, but for me it was also something more. I found myself using what was left of my left hand to play the game, and it became somewhat of an occupational therapy session for me.

My left hand was very sensitive, and everything always felt so weird. When the surgery was performed on my hand, flaps of skin had to be pulled from their normal position to be sutured together, and sometimes brushing the skin in one place caused me to feel it somewhere else. This was also the case with my legs, only much worse. The skin from the back of my calves had been pulled all the way around to the front, and the nerves in that flesh were still very much active. Touching the skin that was now on the front of my leg would cause me to feel it on the back of my leg. It was a very odd feeling, to say the least.

So I now had an outlet for gaming to keep my mind occupied as well as the added bonus of now being able to type comfortably. Writing has always been a simple pleasure of mine. I have written numerous short stories and more than my fair share of poems. A few of those poems have been published online at places like poetry.com, so I can't be a completely awful writer, I suppose. That iPad gave me the opportunity to do some writing and a bit of personal journaling. Several years before, I had started a blog where I would discuss writing projects and trade fiction stories with friends, and I had the sudden urge to return to blogging.

I had so many people that wanted to know how I was doing, and it was hard to keep everyone up to date individually. My parents had to tell the same stories over and over to the clients they saw at the salon and out-of-town family members when they in. A blog seemed like the perfect answer to the problem for me. I could get some writing in, give everyone in my life one central place to see how I was doing, and occasionally vent and rant about my problems. Blogging can be a very therapeutic thing for the mind. It allows you to get all those thoughts - both good and bad - out of your system and into the world. You can tell the world how you feel without ever opening your mouth to anyone, and achieve a much-needed release of your pent-up feelings.

I had found the perfect app to write my blog with, and the right blogging service, but I needed a really good name for the blog and I was drawing a blank. My younger brother Wes would come to the rescue with one of his numerous off-handed comments to me. He and I have always had the type of relationship that thrived on one-upmanship and bickering. An outsider listening in on us going back and forth with each other would be appalled that two brothers could talk to each other in such a way, (our own mother will walk out of the room when we get good and rolling) but for us that's simply how we show we care. Occasionally we both will cross the line, but not very often.

It was during one of these verbal jabbing sessions that my younger brother Wesley gave me the name for my blog. I don't remember exactly what we were ranting about, but I am certain it involved my now short stature. Both of my brothers tower over six feet tall, and I might have been five foot nine inches on a good day before I lost my legs. I was short, and Wes was the tallest of all of us, and that day I must have been complaining about being even shorter than before. I remember ending our little session by saying something similar to, "Well, look at me, I'm at best five feet tall now!"

I had bordered into no-comeback territory for him talking about my lower limbs being gone, and he looked at me funny and turned around and walked out of my room. As far as I was concerned I had just won that round, until of course he stepped back around the corner into my room with a grin on his face.

"You know, Neil, if you think about it, you're really two feet shorter than what you used to be." Ha! that look on his face told me he had just logged himself a little "win" mark on his mental tally board, and I was floored! I didn't feel the least bit hurt by his comment because it was really all in good fun, but he had just given me an awesome name for my blog.

"Dude, two feet shorter! That would make a great name for the blog I am going to start!" Yep, I won that round. My brother gave me a great idea and one more tally mark in my "win" column. I think we both keep marking our points, but we stopped keeping score a long time ago. That's brotherly love for ya.

Christmas had come and gone and I was growing stronger every day. I may not have liked the life I had, but I had to live it regardless and that meant doing my exercises. I spent a lot of time doing leg-lifts and knee-bends, and not having a call button meant I was doing more things on my own. My upper body was gaining back its strength from all the transfers and pushing the wheelchair around, and I found it easier and easier to move myself about with just my arms. I was by no means strong, but at least I was no longer getting worn out by simply rolling across the house to the bathroom.

I hadn't been out of the house since I had come home from the hospital, and New Year's Eve was quickly approaching. The VFW post was having a New Year's Eve dance and everyone seemed to be asking if I was going to come. The VFW has been a big part of all our lives for as long as I could remember, and I have memories of standing next to some of the small round tables in the canteen next to my parents and being so young I could barely see over the top.

From childhood to adulthood I had always gone

there to hang out and to attend functions. I had hunted up Easter eggs many times in the big open field across the parking lot from the old building, and I carried on that tradition with my own son. If you are a veteran and not a member of your local post, I suggest you go take a look. You will never find a greater group of people, or a more supportive group of veterans to help you through your tough times.

As an adult I had spent many a Saturday night taking either dates, wives, or significant others to the monthly dinner and dances, and when I was single I went even more often. I have made some of my best friends close to home on that old hardwood floor in the banquet room, and I have many cherished memories from there. I learned to dance watching my parents out on the dance floor moving to the music of a live band, and I spent many a night on that floor myself trying to emulate my old man's dance moves. Anyone who really knows me knows I love to dance, and the thought of going out to the VFW in a wheelchair was a depressing one.

Depressing or not, I went. I had taken to wearing hats to cover my hair, as an after effect of all the medications I had taken had turned my shiny brown hair into brittle straw. Most days I looked like a scarecrow, so plopping a hat on my head was the easiest thing to do. At home I always wore shorts and t-shirts, as they were the easiest thing to slip into and the most comfortable. My residual limbs were - as always - covered in shrinkers but otherwise exposed at the house, but there was no way I was going to let anyone see them while out at the V. So I struggled into a pair of jeans that were now ridiculously large on me, and I worked long and hard at buttoning on a shirt with only one hand.

Rolling into that old building for the first time since my legs had been taken was a deeply emotional thing for me. Staring at that old hardwood brought forth memories of all the dance partners I had had and all the good times we had made over the years. I saw old friends from high school, buddies I had worked with at the fire department, and friends of the family that had literally watched me grow up in that very building.

I spent the entire night in my wheelchair, pant legs stereotypically tucked up under my thighs, trying my best to smile at everyone and show them that I was still alive and fighting. I saw many friends that night and I am very glad that I made the short trip to the VFW for that New Year's Eve dance, as that would be the last year-end ever celebrated in that old hall. Across the parking lot in the big open field where I had once chased after Easter eggs sat a new building, not quite ready to move into. The old building was nearly sixty years old and had seen better days, but the Men's Auxiliary had worked very hard raising funds to get a new building started.

I lasted about two and a half hours that night before I was totally exhausted and I was home and in bed before the clock came close to striking midnight. I spent the end of the worst year of my life, and the beginning of the toughest and most rewarding year of my life fast asleep. Happy New Year, indeed.

17 - TALL

Things really began to move as the new year dawned, and I was ready for anything that would get me out of my chair. I was ready for some hope. I was still coming to terms with who I was now and what had happened to me, and I began to feel as if I were in a holding pattern. Every day became a monotony of sitting, exercising, rolling, and television and internet consumption. That was all I had to do with my time, all I was physically capable of doing.

I now scoured the internet for information about limb loss the way I had once scoured it for information about Behcet's Disease. Somewhere out there was information that would help me get better, information that would help me live again and I was bound and determined to find it. I found very quickly that there was not much hope for my left hand, as a partial hand amputee who still has residual digits like I had didn't have any good options for prosthetics. There would be no cool myo-electric hand for me. My best hope were some fake latex fingers I could glue on every morning. I didn't want that, I wanted my hand back! So, I kept looking.

I read a lot of blogs and a lot of horror stories about people with less amputations than I had who just could not walk anymore, their prosthesis hurt so they stayed in a wheelchair. I held onto Matt Hayden's promise of 98%, and I trusted that he would come through for me when it was time. One of my problems was that I didn't know when the time would come, as the dreaded "hurry up and wait" had once again struck.

I had gotten tired of answering untold amounts of messages, emails, phone calls and texts, so I made the decision to start my blog, and by the middle of January I had made my first post, documenting my experiences and how I was feeling. I would like to say that I was just too tired to talk to everyone individually, but I simply didn't want to talk to much of anyone. I didn't mind visits so much, but I would cringe every time the phone rang. No one would leave me alone, and that was really what I wanted.

I was falling into a state of depression, and whenever I talked to my family, or my friends visited, I put on a happy face. The happy face hid what was growing on the inside, namely a self-loathing and slow burning rage about what had happened to me. During the day I had to be happy, but the late nights were all my own to brood, as sleep does not come easy to a new amputee.

When you lose a limb the brain doesn't understand, it tries to talk to the part of the body that is no longer there and it gets no response. So, the brain does what anyone else does when it really needs to talk to someone in a bad way - it keeps calling. When it still doesn't get an answer, it will begin to yell. Repeatedly. The sensation is similar for a lot of amputees, and I have always called it "buzzing."

Imagine holding a hornet's nest in your arms and shaking it up, getting those critters inside all good and angry. Don't worry- they can't get out of the nest. So they just keep on buzzing angrily around inside, bouncing off the walls and causing a major racket. That is the sensation I was feeling in the ends of my residual limbs, a constant buzzing. No medications could control it, and during the day when I was keeping my mind busy and occupied I didn't need it to be controlled. Night time, on the other hand, was a different story.

When the house was quiet and I was lying in bed, my brain would continue to yell at my non-existent calves and feet through the severed tin-cans-and-string of my nervous system. It kept calling, and nobody was home. My legs would keep me awake all night long with the buzzing, and I spent many a morning watching the sky outside grow bright with sunlight through the bedroom window. I was being slowly tortured by my own body, being deprived of sleep. There is only so much of this a man can take before his thoughts grow dark, and mine grew as black as my fingers had once been.

Every night I would lay in bed staring at the ceiling fan above my head going round and round, and I began to have one thought go round and around in my head to match it. I should have died. My nightly overpowering thought became that if only I had died I wouldn't have to live like this now. I wouldn't have to be this legless freak that couldn't do anything but eat, sleep, and shit. It wasn't my fault I was this way, I hadn't asked for it, I didn't agree to any of this. No, I wasn't the one that agreed to the treatment that would take my legs. If the doctors had been able to wake me up and ask *me* if I wanted to live like this, I would have said *hell no*, but I wasn't consulted.

No, my family was consulted, and their answer was

we don't care if he loses all his limbs, as long as we get to keep him. A rage was growing inside me because the decision to live like this was taken from me and given to family members that I now only saw as selfish fools. Nobody asked me if I wanted to live like this, they made the choice for me, and I began to hate my family for damning me to a life without limbs and all it entailed.

I spent so many nights wailing into my pillow so no one in the house would hear me crying out my anger and resentment, and mourning the loss of my legs and my fingers. I would spend my days growing distant from my parents and my brothers, doing my best to avoid talking to any of them. All I could see when I looked at them were pariahs, and they might as well have had "selfish" tattooed onto their foreheads, because that's all I could think of them when I saw them. Selfish people that chose to let me live broken like this so they wouldn't have to suffer the loss of a son or brother. I was made to suffer because of their selfishness.

My room became my refuge, and I spent most of my time there, away from the world and these people I had grown to hate. I tolerated visits to my room to check on me, and I began to distinguish who was coming simply by the sound of the steps. I would close my eyes and feign sleep when I could, and when I couldn't I would answer "I'm ok" to the inevitable question of how I was doing. But I wasn't ok, I was slowly losing it inside my own head and secretly wishing I would die, because I had begun to hate myself as much as I hated my family for allowing me to live.

I don't think I could have ever acted on that wish,

and luckily for my tortured psyche I was never given a chance. I had been up for several days in a row unable to sleep, catching naps for an hour here and there during the day when total exhaustion overpowered the buzzing and tingling in my distal ends. Night came and I once again began my ritual of television, internet surfing, and eventual breakdown into pitiful sobbing over what I had become.

My little office-turned-bedroom happened to share a bathroom with my parent's bedroom. If I needed a drink of water, an extra pillow or blanket, or anything else all I had to do was yell for my mother and she would be there. Since I was a little boy I have instinctively known the sound volume to wake my parents from a dead sleep, by either staying up past bedtime or screaming in the night from a nightmare. I think all children must know this, because my son could wake me from a dead sleep from his room when he was little if he needed me, but could be quiet as a mouse when he was up late playing while he was supposed to be sleeping.

I had just begun my nightly trip through hell, continually asking myself how my family could have been this selfish, how they couldn't have thought about what I would want, and wondering why I had to survive at all - when my mother decided to make a late night trip to that adjoining bathroom. She must have heard me sobbing into my pillow because suddenly she was there, climbing into the bed with me and holding me, rocking me as if I were a scared child. I was a scared child- her child- and I was also angry. All those sleepless nights full of pent up rage came boiling out at me when she asked me what was wrong. I finally exploded, I finally let it out.

I told my mother how selfish she and everyone else had been to make this choice for me. I told her it wasn't fair and I didn't want to live like this, I didn't ask to live like this, and it was all their faults. I spoke my rage until it was all out, and my dear and patient mother let me. I wailed and cried and said ugly things, and she just kept on hugging me and rocking. She kept on while I cursed her and dad, my brothers Kyle and Wes, and the decision they all made.

And she never let go of me, not even when her own tears started falling.

When I finally came to the end of all my rage what my mother told me was so simple, and it shamed me for all my horrible thoughts. *We love you, Tyler loves you, and we didn't want to lose you. Yes, that may seem selfish, but you were fighting so hard to live we thought you wanted to. We thought you would want to live!* She said many other things to me, but those were the words that stuck. She was right, and I knew it. I had never backed down from any fight, so they assumed I wouldn't want to back down from this one, either.

I was being the selfish one, by projecting my own misery and self-pity onto them and being angry about what had happened. It was no one's fault, it just happened. And I accepted that fact as I sat on my bed with my mother hugging me while we both cried. I accepted it. I bought it. I paid for it. And then I owned it. I had just hit rock bottom, and now it was time to start climbing back out, legs or not. I was horrible to my mother that night, and I wasn't quiet about it. I don't know if my dad woke up to hear any of that, but if he did he has never said a word to me about it. I hope he slept through it all, because he raised all of his sons to be good men, not the petulant child I had become that night.

I started my climb out of that pit without legs, but we soon got a phone call that would change that. Matt Hayden was ready to get started on my legs, and it was time to take a trip back to Louisville.

Kentucky Prosthetics is on a small side street in downtown Louisville, sitting squarely in the shadow of the Jewish/U of L hospital complex. That first car ride back to Louisville was an exciting ride for me, and my head was a-swim with the possibilities. I had it firmly in my head that I would strap those legs on and be walking in days, but that's not quite how it went down.

We lived three hours away and my parents worked, so weekends were our only real option. Matt didn't bat an eye over taking up an entire Sunday to work with me, so we headed out early one Sunday morning that January to meet him at his office. I was unsure what exactly would happen or even how I would be fitted with my new legs, but Matt explained it all as he went.

The office is laid out much like a doctor's office, with exam rooms, reception windows, and a waiting room filled with reading materials by the chairs and children's toys in a corner. The room I was wheeled into was a casting room, and in that room I had my first taste of the process I knew I would have to continue for the rest of my life.

Having your distal ends cast is in some ways very similar to having a cast put on a broken limb, except that the goal is to keep the cast intact when it is removed. That casting is a snapshot of your limb, detailing every bone structure, land mark, and protuberance on the limb. The casting material is even regular casting tape used to mend fractures, and having that wet and warm tape wrapped around my very sensitive legs was an experience. Matt skillfully wrapped both my residual limbs in layers and layers of the stuff, working it with his hands until it had captured the exact shape of them.

I had to sit in my wheelchair with my knees locked out and legs fully extended until the tape dried. My limbs had been wrapped in a tubular plastic bag to keep the tape from sticking to my skin, but it sure didn't seem to help when it came time to pull those castings off. The legs were done one at a time, so twice I felt like I was going to be yanked out of my chair as Matt worked the dried castings off my legs. It was a painful and totally foreign experience for me, but I set my jaw and let it happen. If I wanted to walk again, this was part of it. The process of making prosthetic limbs is lengthy, and especially so when you are a two-for-one special such as myself. We were going to have to stay in Louisville overnight, and Matt was kind enough to make sure we would have a hotel room. Those castings he had just taken needed to be turned into molds of my limbs which would eventually be made into sockets, but the process would take some time, so Matt sent us over to the hotel to get settled in.

We stayed right down on the riverfront at the Galt House- twin towers connected by an enclosed bridge-way that I had stayed at many times in the past while working in Louisville. It is not too far from Fourth Street, which is a downtown party central with rows upon rows upon levels of bars, pubs, and clubs. I had spent more than one night with co-workers and friends on pub crawls there, having staggered back to the Galt in the wee hours of the morning. I even know a girl who was conceived at that hotel, as her proud father is a good friend of mine and I watched her grow up. Needless to say, I am familiar with the place.

As familiar as I was, I had never experienced it from a wheelchair. The accommodations were fine, and the handicapped accessible things worked well for me, but I didn't want to have to use them, I didn't want to be handicapped. I wanted to walk again, and that was why we were here.

The room had two beds, and they were tall and comfortable. My folks laid out for a nap, but I was too keyed up to sleep. I was waiting for a phone call, and when it came it would mean it was time for me to go walk again. Again. I had done it all my life, and I was so ready to start doing it again. So, it was more of "hurry up and wait." Matt had to take the plaster castings of my legs and turn them into plastic sockets that would be attached to my new legs and feet.

My one comfort was the shiny new liners I was wearing on my legs, and I didn't want to take them off. Liners are part of the interface system between the residual limb and the prosthesis, and are the equivalent of a thick silicone sock, except mine were made of polyurethane. They fit snuggly on the ends of my legs, and for the first time since my amputations, the angry hornet's nest inside my legs grew quiet - the liners had calmed them down. Putting them on for the first time was a chore, and my sensitive limbs protested, but once they had settled into place I was in a desensitized heaven.

So I sat on the hotel room bed and waited,

watching the TV with the volume on low, and snapping the edges of my liners on the top of my thighs like a rubber band. It would be several hours before the call would come, but it finally did. Matt Hayden had come into the office on a Sunday for me and worked his ass off to get my first set of legs ready for me to try. I had a hard time containing my excitement as we wheeled down to the car, and I practically jumped across that slide board into the front seat. I think my father had to tell me to calm down because I was so excited, but even he couldn't blame me. We were all a bit excited about what was about to happen, we all wanted to see me stand up and walk.

The patient rooms aren't much like any other place I have been, except possibly a physical therapy gym. The rooms are long and slim, leaving just enough room to walk on either side of a set of therapy walking bars. Shelves and cubby holes abound with various types of prosthesis, and the walls are covered with posters and photos of Paralympic medalists and amputee success stories, all whom are patients of Kentucky Prosthetics. Sitting in my wheelchair at the head of those bars, with the smiling faces of other amputees who were living their lives looking down at me from the walls, I was both terrified and elated.

Matt was in the back shop working on my first set of test legs, and my family and I were tense waiting for that moment when we would see them for the first time. When Matt finally appeared with my new lease on life in his hands my heart was pounding. They seemed so enormous and tall, and looked nothing like what I had expected. Both had a clear set of plastic sockets on top, and feet at the bottom covered by the last pair of shoes I had ever worn on my own long-gone feet. I expected a simple pipe connecting those two components much as I had seen on legs I had researched online, but what was mounted in between those sockets and feet was entirely different.

Instead of a simple pylon pipe there was a larger diameter cylindrical contraption with a hard rubber flange and black hoses coming from it, connected to the socket. Matt explained this new component as an "elevated vacuum system" called the Harmony P3, and these things were going to keep me in the socket and help my residual limbs stay healthy. The system would work by pumping a small amount of air out of the socket with every step, allowing for greater contact and less air while I was wearing the prosthesis. It would add a bit of weight to the legs as a whole, but because of the better fit I would have, I wouldn't notice the weight. All I could do was trust Matt. He had promised me 98%, and these Harmony pumps were a part of the plan to get me back to living.

Slipping the legs on for the first time was a task, as they were a near-perfect form fit for my limbs and we had to press my legs down inside. There were outer sleeves on the sockets which had to be reflected and pulled up over my thighs, and the very first thing I noticed when lifting my leg to allow the sleeve to come up was the weight of the prosthetic on my leg as a whole. It felt so *heavy*! The next thing I noticed was an abrupt center-of-gravity change while sitting in my wheelchair. I had just spent the last three months sitting down with nothing touching the floor, and a center of gravity somewhere around mid-chest level. As soon as both of my prosthetic feet touched the floor, my center of gravity snapped back to my waist!

It was an incredible feeling, being able to support even my seated weight with full legs on the floor, and I felt a constant tension I never realized I had relaxing from my upper body. I had spent so much time seated without legs that I had been making constant small adjustments to stay upright- I had been a weeble-wobble. Now with feet on the floor I was a biped once again and all the tension in my back, shoulders, hips, and thighs melted away. I felt normal for the first time in months! Matt made minor adjustments and asked me questions about how the sockets felt and fit, and when he was satisfied with everything it was time for me to stand up.

It took me several tries to stand even with using the therapy bars as handholds, and Matt finally had to grip me about the waist and give me a boost up onto my legs. All thoughts of conquering walking in a few days immediately dissipated as I stood on those legs for the first time. The pressure on my legs was intense, everything felt funny and off, and my lower back was throbbing with pain. I was standing, but it wasn't nearly as easy or fun as I had expected. My prosthetist checked over a few things, and then thankfully let me sit back down. I was covered in sweat from just that first short minute up on my new legs, and I was shaking a bit from the exertion.

Matt was soon ready to have me up again, and this time I had to walk. My father was behind my wheelchair, and was at the ready so he could follow me down the bars for the first time. We got me standing up once again, and it was now time for me to take that first step. I was weak, my balance was horrible, and I hung on to the bars for dear life, but I took that first step. That first step would become the second greatest accomplishment in my life behind becoming a father. Raising that prosthetic leg off the floor just a fraction of an inch and putting my weight on the other leg was exquisite torture, and getting that raised leg forward and down again was as close as I will ever get to moving a mountain. But I did it. I had taken that first step!

The second and third steps were not much easier, but I made them as well. I eventually made it down the ten foot length of bars, step by laborious step, and I practically collapsed into my wheelchair when I was done. I made a few more short trips down the bars that day, with Matt following along in front of me, my father behind, and my mother to the side playing videographer and cheering section. Matt would occasionally stop me and make marks on my sockets, drawing circles and dashes and writing in a form of short-hand that only his mind could comprehend, in preparation of final socket and alignment adjustments.

We were sent back to the hotel for the night, with plans to reconvene testing in the morning. That night I slept better than I had in months, I was exhausted, and the pressure in the sockets had made those hornets' nests in my legs calm down for the first time in ages. The next morning was a slow and easy one at the hotel, and we had breakfast in the hotel restaurant overlooking the Ohio River. I ate my eggs and gazed out across the water, thinking about all the water rescue operations I had worked on that very waterway downriver, and for the first time realized that I might just get to do it again. I had walked, and that gave me true hope, hope that I could do all the things I loved to do again. Those things, my 98%, my fire and rescue work, my motorcycle riding, my Jiu Jitsu training, and even the simple things like taking my son fishing were all on my mind when we arrived back at that little office in the shadow of Jewish Hospital the next day.

It was now Monday, and the quiet office I had been in the day before was now a bustling and busy prosthetics office. We met the office staff, including Matt's wife Diana, and what I would eventually refer to as my prosthetic team. Sienna Newman, an extraordinary prosthetist and amputee advocate, was introduced to me and my parents, as well as Tommy and Mike. Tommy is a certified prosthetist who both sees patients and builds limbs in the shop, and Mike is the resident mechanic who spends most of his time in the back crafting the limbs Matt, Sienna, and Tommy cast and design.

Matt gave me the run of the office that day, and I got to spend plenty of time in the back shop hanging out and watching the art of prosthetic making. Because both Tommy and Mike had spent so much time around amputees, I was nothing more than a regular person to them. We talked sports, motorcycles (Mike's a Harley guy) and guns. The entire time I was there I never felt like I was being looked at with pity or horror and for the first time since my amputations I felt like just a regular guy around strangers. To this day when I go in to get work done I go in the back and talk prosthetics, bikes, rifles and handguns with Mike, and shoot the breeze with Tommy.

I sat and watched as my legs had final adjustments

put to them, and then wheeled back into an exam room, ready to head down the bars once more. All those hieroglyphs Matt had put on the clear sockets the day before had been turned into tweaks and changes that would add much comfort and fit for me. Getting the legs on the second day was a bit easier than the previous, and I soon found myself once again standing with Matt in front, Dad behind, and Mom to the side documenting everything with a camera.

As I took those slow steps down the bar I thought again about all those things I had thought about over breakfast, and I talked about doing them again. I told Matt and my parents I was going to ride a motorcycle again, that I was going to get back on a fire engine and that I was going to get back on the Jiu Jitsu mat. That last one caused Matt to raise an eyebrow and tell me, "I don't know about that one."

All I could tell him was, "You just watch me!"

Matt can seem very deadpan, and it took me a long time to get his dry humor and reserved expressions. I still don't know if he was simply prodding me good-naturedly with his comment, or if he truly meant it. I do know that it became a motivator for me, as with so many other things I had done in my life, to prove him or anyone else wrong when I was told something couldn't be done. I don't often back down from a challenge, and I took his words as such.

I finished up my last walking session of the day, and for my family and myself it was a very emotional experience. The thing that we had worked so hard for since I had woken from my coma had just happened. I had walked again! I had beaten the odds, stood, and taken those first steps into a new life. One thing that was readily apparent to me was that I couldn't stand up straight. My months stuck in a rolling prison had shaped and molded my body into a seated position, and that was the cause of the lower back pain I had felt the day before.

Even though I stood with a slightly bent posture, one thing was very clear to me as I looked at myself in the full-length mirror I faced at the end of the bars. I was towering over my father's six foot frame by several inches. I had always been the shortest of my brothers, but not anymore. I was tall for the first time in my life, and I was standing on my own two feet.

The ride home from Louisville was a bittersweet one. I had got into my new legs for the first time and walked, and no sooner than I got them, they were taken away again. The clear plastic check-sockets are not really safe for everyday use, and Matt needed them to make a carbon fiber set that I could use every day. He gave me a new and smaller set of shrinkers, and I felt it was not an even trade. New shrinkers meant more adjustments, and getting used to smaller compression socks is a literal pain. Regardless of the pain of new shrinks, I put them on. They are an integral part of the process, and I would do everything I needed to do so I could have a normal life again.

Now home again we all tried to get back into a routine, but at least for a short while that was not to be. After everything my poor family had been through with me, tragedy struck us once again. My grandmother - my mother's mother - passed away, leaving a large hole in the hearts of us all. It wasn't unexpected as she was getting on in years and had been dealing with steadily declining health, but it was a fierce blow to my mother after everything she had just been through with me.

Grandmother (yes, all of us kids called her Grandmother, not Me-maw, Ma-ma, or Granny) had retired to Florida years ago, but had a burial plot beside my grandfather in central Indiana. He died a few months before I was born so I never got to meet him, but I am told I have many of his mannerisms. The funeral was to be in Terre Haute, Indiana, and I was simply not up for making the trip or seeing family while sitting in a wheelchair, so we all made the decision for me to stay home alone.

I hadn't spent the night alone since mom had picked me up from Bowling Green, and she was concerned about it. I, of course, had no doubts I could handle myself for a day without anyone around, and I was looking forward to some true peace and quiet.

My folks left before daylight on the day of the funeral, so I awoke to an empty house. I had promised my mother I would eat, but I don't think she believed me. She had been fixing my plates and bringing me coffee since I had come home from the hospital, and she was afraid I would starve before they got back home. When I rolled into the kitchen that morning I had to smile, as piled on the kitchen table and on the seats of chairs was every ready-to-eat packaged food imaginable. My mother, on the morning she would have to go lay her mother to rest, was still thinking about me starving. There were bags of potato chips, canned soup, snacks of all kinds, and plates, bowls, and utensils sitting within easy reach for me. All I had to do was brew my own coffee.

What can I say? I'm a momma's boy, and my

momma loves me.

My parents made it back home late the next day, and life in the Brown house slowly returned to normal. The grief from losing Grandmother lingered, but we all did our best to cope and continue on. My grandmother was a great, strong, forceful woman who loved life and loved her children and grandchildren. She would be sorely missed.

18 - WAITING

Everyone was home, road trips were over for a while, and everything returned to as normal as it could be for a guy with no legs. I was alone much of the day while my parents were at work and alone all night after they went to bed. I still couldn't sleep for my legs constantly buzzing, and boredom began to set in. Between my brother Wes and my son, an Xbox console was found and set up in my room for me. I could now watch television on the flat screen with it, and I tried my hand at gaming with a controller to relieve my boredom.

When my son had been much younger we had connected often with online gaming during the weekdays when he was at his mom's house. I couldn't see him in person, but I could go online and get into a game party with him and play games. It was a good way for me to keep in touch, have an impact on his life, and meet his friends at the same time. If you ever want to know what kind of language an early teen uses, join their Xbox Live party. His buddies would forget I was there and then pop off with some rather imaginative curse words, and follow immediately with "Sorry Mr. Brown!"

My boy and I began to game that way again in those days before I got my new legs. It was good for us both, because it was so normal. He was only able

166

to make it there to see me every other weekend, so hanging out online and shooting bad guys on Call of Duty was the next best thing. I had really missed my kiddo while I was away in Louisville and catching up on time either in person or online was a good thing for us both. The kid watched his father nearly die and then lose his legs, so he needed to hang out with me as much as I needed to hang out with him.

Other than hangin' with the boy, all I was really doing was killing time until my legs arrived. Even after they arrived I wasn't supposed to do anything until I could get into gait training and therapy, but I had become accustomed to waiting. I spent my time updating my blog, reading lots of books, and continuing my leg exercises. I also made it a point to join some online amputee groups so I could see how other people cope, and ask questions of veterans of limb loss.

I found out many interesting things chatting in those groups, and both gave and received really good information. I also learned very quickly that amputees can be very bitter people, and that I did not want to be like that. I may have lost my legs and fingers but I didn't have to let it rule my world. So I made it a point to limit my interactions with those who could not get past their own limb loss.

I would get occasional updates from Matt and Sienna on the progress of my new legs, and nearly three weeks after my trip to Louisville I was told my legs were on their way! I don't think amputees normally get their new prosthetics via UPS, but being as I was three hours away, an exception was made. I spent a lot of time sitting by the door waiting for that big brown truck to pull in the drive, and when it finally did I braved the February cold to somehow lug the big box in while sitting in my wheelchair. It just happened to be the 14th, so it was a very happy Valentine's Day for me!

You can unbox all the new phones and electronic toys you want. It will never be better than unboxing your own legs for the first time. The clear plastic check sockets had been replaced with black carbon fiber, and these legs were much more lightweight than the test legs had been. I was told to simply put them on and get used to having them on my residual limbs, and to not try to walk in them. Yea, that didn't last long.

I put those legs on right there in the kitchen. I wasn't silly enough to try and walk with no one in the house, but that wouldn't keep me from doing what I was supposed to do, which was get used to wearing prosthetics. Sitting in the wheelchair with legs on still felt odd, as my center of gravity shifted lower once again, and looking down at my feet while sitting in my chair led to an amazing discovery. I discovered post haste that my brain was an idiot.

I had never experienced much in the way of true phantom pain in my limbs, my amputations weren't from direct trauma, and my body had a chance to get used to the idea that my legs were gone before they were actually taken off. The buzzy feeling really isn't phantom, either. It is simply nerve bundles freaking out over a lost connection. When I looked down at my feet in that wheelchair, all I could see was the tops of my knees and the ends of my shoes, and I could move those shoes around a bit.

My eyes told my brain that they were seeing feet again, and the brain said *Wonderful! I have been wanting to talk to those two!* My brain saw feet, and then proceeded to torture me with the weirdness of phantom pain. I would get cramps in big toes that were no longer there, or the top of my foot would suddenly begin to itch horribly and I couldn't scratch it. The absolute worst was the cramp in the arch of my right foot, always the right. I couldn't massage it out and there was no way to stretch anything to relieve the cramp. I just had to clench my jaw and work through the pain.

Stupid brain.

The process seems mystical, the thought of feeling limbs that are no longer there, but in reality it is fairly simple. The brain and nervous system are a collection of wires that electrical impulses ride around on. And much like a telephone line, the brain will put in a call to a particular part of the body, and that body part picks up the phone and responds. Phantom pain happens when the brain puts in a call - say, to my nonexistent feet - and it doesn't get an answer. The brain might hang up and try the call again, and still no response. Eventually the brain will get frustrated at the constant dial-tone, and decide to turn into a stalking ex-girlfriend.

Instead of a simple phone call, the brain might order the nervous system to do a quick drive-by and see if anyone is home, possibly causing an itch or two. Of course, there is no response, so the stalker ex-girlfriend of a brain decides to up the ante a bit, calls up its BFF, the nervous system, to ask it to pull in the driveway and knock on the door. So comes the big toe cramp. Doesn't matter how much the nerves knock on the door, no one is home. The brain then decides to go ballistic and just burn the whole house down, and there are your major pains and cramps.

Amputees of traumatic accidents whose last experience with the limb was extreme pain often complain of constantly re-living that pain in a phantom limb. Some studies suggest that the pain is a result of the brain and nervous system not being able to let go of the experience, or simply being "locked in" to the last thing that limb felt. Luckily, this isn't much of a problem for me.

Nope, my brain was just an idiot and a stalker.

Eventually my nervous system gave up, and the phantoms went away, but for a few weeks at least my brain was trying to rekindle a lost romance with a pair of feet that had skipped town. All because I saw feet sticking out below my knees.

Having my legs at home with me meant that at every opportunity I was trying to walk. My mother borrowed a walker from a client, and we all spent many a night in the kitchen with me practicing standing up and sitting back down. Having no calf muscles meant all my standing had to be done with leverage, momentum, and upper body strength. The walker helped with balance, as I couldn't yet even stand without holding onto something.

I eventually moved on from a simple stand to slowly scooting my way around the kitchen floor, one laborious step at a time. Even picking my feet up enough to step was extremely hard. Walking in bars is one thing. The bars give you much more in the way of stability and balance. Walking with a walker was something else entirely. I just didn't yet have the strength to take more than a few steps. Having been in a hospital bed and then a wheelchair for so long had turned my upper legs to jello, so I started doing the thing that had made my legs so strong before all this happened; I started crawling again.

Out of my seventeen year career in the pest control industry, at least twelve of those years were spent crawling underneath houses and buildings. In my time I have crawled under the homes of country music stars, NCAA championship basketball coaches, United States Congressmen, and even crawled under a few professional baseball legends' homes. I have encountered everything from protective raccoon mothers to angry timber rattlesnakes. I didn't crawl every single day, but a good average would be at least three houses a day for those twelve years. That adds up to somewhere around *six hundred miles* of crawling on my hands and knees in the dirt and muck.

I thought crawling around the house wearing kneepads would be a breeze. I was wrong. Totally wrong. No amount of exercises will prepare you for using muscles that have had nearly five months to atrophy. It was a struggle in the beginning, but clomping around the house down on all fours did more to prepare me for my eventual gait training than anything else. It also gave me a little bit of freedom from the chair. I was mobile again without aid, and everyone in the house had to watch out so they wouldn't step on me.

When the folks would leave for work I would explore the house from a totally new perspective, and would try all kinds of things that would have otherwise freaked them out. I would climb into the kitchen chairs, just to see if I could make it up and down. I would make a run at the stairs leading to the second floor, although I never made it all the way up. My dad has a roll around office chair at a desk right off the kitchen, and I even made it into that. I did discover rather quickly that without feet you have no way of controlling where one of those roll, and I ended up stuck for half an hour in a corner of the kitchen trying to get back out of the thing!

Crawling on my hands and knees also gave me more options for taking showers and getting clean. I couldn't stand showering in a shower chair because it felt so unsafe, but crawling into a stand up shower and sitting down in the floor gave me the first relaxing shower I had had in months! All I had to worry about was reaching the faucet controls, and making sure I didn't sit on the drain. My success in the shower led me to try something else I had been unable to do for months - I discovered I could empty my bladder without having to sit down on the toilet.

I was alone in the house and after my normal full pot of coffee one morning I really had to go. My options were to climb into my chair and go all the way across the house to my handicap bathroom, or make a go for my parents' bathroom the next room over. The urgency of my bladder convinced me to crawl right next door where I had to sit down in the floor just to figure out the logistics of going to the bathroom while standing on my knees.

If you have a son or little boy in the house, you well know the posture they use when they finally learn to go "potty like a big boy." They drop their pants completely to the floor and then tuck their shirt up under their chin before they do the deed. I never quite understood why little boys did that until I was presented with the problem of trying to pee into a toilet bowl that is almost at waist level to me. Now I totally dig why they do it, and that is exactly what I ended up doing. I have no balance while trying to stand up on my knees so I had to hold onto the wall for support, but I was able to go to the bathroom standing up, on my own, for the first time in months.

Believe it or not, this was a very emotional thing for me. I had been sitting down to urinate for *months*, and it was driving me to frustration. So there I was with my pants down around my knees and shirt tucked under my chin in front of the toilet getting all emotional over finally getting to pee like a normal guy again. well, sort of normal, anyway. I cried right then and there. Not the most manly thing, I know, but I was alone and I could be emotional if I wanted.

Except I wasn't alone.

My dad had a habit of coming home during breaks in his day to check on me, and normally I could hear his truck pull up and then the old wrought-iron back door slam shut when he or anyone else came in the house. Not that day, oh no. My old man pulled some mad ninja skills out of his hat that morning, and as I was kneeled down there with my hind-end in the breeze whooping and hollering over my newfound bathroom skills my dad appeared right beside me thinking I was hurt - or worse.

I didn't even realize he was there until he asked, "what's the matter!? Are you ok?!" If my bladder wasn't already empty I would have made a mess on the floor his sudden appearance had surprised me so much! All I could do was sheepishly grin and tell him, "I just peed standing up for the first time!"

He seemed rather nonplussed as he told me, "Well, good for you, son," and then walked out of the bathroom and made for the back of the house. That's my old man, nothing fazes him. I was rather proud of myself as I pulled up my drawers and made my way back to my room. Good for me, indeed.

Between the crawling and the leg exercises my thigh muscles began to strengthen and I began to be more aggressive with my walker-assisted steps. Every night we would all gather in the kitchen after my parents got home from work and they would cheer me on as I progressed from walking from chair to chair around the table, then from kitchen to hallway, and eventually from the back of the house all the way to my room. I can make it from my part of the house to the back door in about ten seconds now, but that first attempt took me twenty minutes, with several rest stops in between. That final walk was a hard won victory for me, and I knew I was nearly ready for my gait training. As it would turn out, the strength in my legs wouldn't be my toughest obstacle to overcome in getting back to physical therapy. No, my tallest hurdle would be insurance.

19 - ADVOCATE

There is a great gap in this country between the prosthetic care that amputees need and the care and services that their health insurance will actually pay for. A book could be written all by itself about prosthetic fairness or parity, and all the things insurance companies will do to get out of paying for anything more than a basic leg or arm. Some insurance gives you the opportunity to either get a new leg or a new wheelchair, but not both. As far as the insurance world is concerned, a prosthetic limb is nothing more than a mobility appliance, not unlike a crutch, so why should they pay for two different types of crutches?

I know it seems totally backwards, but that is the way major medical coverage sees things. They also want to give you the most basic appliance necessary, with the thought that if you can walk from the bathroom to the bedroom or from the living room to the refrigerator you have all you need. Practically every amputee goes through this fight to a certain extent, and some more than others. If prosthetic companies still carved legs from oak and willow wood, insurance companies would fight to keep amputees in them.

I had been put on short term disability for work, which kept me in a paycheck as well as kept my health coverage in force. This was a life saver for me, because my three month hospital stint racked up more than a half million dollars in medical expenses, and my insurance paid a large portion of those bills. When it came to my prosthetics, though, they were saying no at every turn. My Harmony P3 pumps were considered too high tech for my needs, and I received letter after letter from them stating why they were turning down my claim for this particular type of suspension device.

According to my insurance, all I needed was a simple SACH foot (Solid Ankle, Cushioned Heel) and a steel pipe to mount it on. Insurance was turning down claims on the *legs I was already wearing!* Matt and Sienna were re-filing constantly, trying to explain why I might need something a little better, considering that I was a bilateral below knee amputee who wanted to do more than make it to the fridge and the bathroom, but insurance kept saying no. My prosthetic gurus told me they wouldn't stop until we got approval, but things were looking a bit grim from my perspective. I did not want my legs taken away, and I was getting worried.

Since I had gotten home from the hospital I had been receiving an occasional phone call and email from someone with my insurance company who called herself my "case worker." She was the person that reviewed all the paperwork, all the hospital documentation, and my records and then sent it all up the chain to the doctor who would make the decisions as to what the insurance would pay for.

My case worker was always nice and pleasant, but I didn't much pay attention to our brief correspondence in the beginning. I know I told her I was excited about getting to walk again, and had told her about starting my blog, but our conversations before my first castings were brief. To me she was simply a polite nurse who worked for the enemy of an insurance company I had, but I couldn't have been more mistaken. My case worker turned out to be a friend, a gatekeeper, and a fan of my blog.

After the second time my legs were turned down, she and I had a long phone conversation about it, and I really opened up to her about my fears of having my legs taken away and not being able to get back to living my life. From that moment on she started really working for me and advocating for me and the legs I wanted.

We began having near weekly phone calls, where I would update her on my progress with my walking, tell her about all the stupid stunts I would pull, and talk about life in general. She would cheer on my efforts, tell me how much she enjoyed keeping up with me on my blog, and give me advice about the little things that I was having problems with concerning my health. Outside of our conversations my case worker-turned-friend was churning out paperwork, bending doctors' ears, and making just enough of a racket for me on her end of things that these legs that the insurance had told me I didn't need were suddenly approved! My advocate had come through for me in a big way, and even making a point to call and tell me I was going to get to keep my legs before the acceptance letter had been put in the mail. She worked hard to get me what I wanted because she believed in me, and knew that I believed in myself. The first hurdle in getting to rehab and gait training had been cleared, but there would be more to come, and my case worker would be there again to back me up.

My short term disability was very close to expiring, and that meant my insurance would be as well. I did not pick up long-term disability from work because I had felt it was something I would never actually have to use. I had less than two months to get my gait training scheduled and completed, as well as find prosthetic fingers that might work for me. I was running out of time.

Insurance wanted me to go to a less expensive outpatient facility close to home, and my prosthetics team wanted me back at Frazier Rehab Institute so I could be close to them as well as get full time inpatient care and therapy. I wasn't a single leg amputee who had a "sound leg" to rely on, I was a triple amputee who had sever atrophy and needed intense all day therapy and nightly after-care. The facilities near me simply would not cut it.

There were plenty of places close to home that could take care of triage therapy for me, but I would never learn to walk by sitting in a chair and throwing a ball back and forth with a PTA for three hours a week. That was the care the insurance company wanted to have, as it would be less costly. I was having none of it, though.

At the same time as we were rushing to get me to a facility while I still had coverage, I was scouring every source I could to find the best possible prosthetic fingers for my poor left hand. I had too much in the way of digits to have a microprocessor controlled hand, and I didn't want glued-on silicone fingers that were purely cosmetic. I needed to find body powered digits that would work for my hand, and my options were limited.

I eventually discovered a device called the X Fingers on a YouTube video of a national newscast. A man by the name of Dan Didrick had created a complex body powered finger that could be easily applied to the types of residual digits I had, and I wanted a set. The look on Matt and Sienna's faces was a bit skeptical when I gave them the information about these new fingers that they had never seen, but they looked into them for me regardless. The X Fingers were expensive, to say the least, and insurance companies all over were refusing to pay for such a new type of prosthetic. My prosthetic team went ahead and cast my hand and made the contacts needed to get the ball rolling on my new fingers, and then that ball would be put into my insurance company's court.

My regular calls with my case worker were still going like clockwork, and I was blogging about these new fingers I wanted to try. Since she had still been reading my blog, she was up to speed on my happenings. We'd had such a long fight trying to get my legs processed and approved that I was stunned when the X Fingers were approved the first time Kentucky Prosthetics sent in the paperwork. I had my case worker to thank, and as soon as the request came across her desk she took it straight to the insurance company doctor who makes prosthetic approvals and told him to sign it. I needed those fingers and she wanted me to have them, so she got it done for me.

It would be several months before I would receive my completed set of fingers, but with insurance approval taken care of I had no worries about them being paid for. My case manger had come through for me, and she wasn't done yet; I still had inpatient therapy that needed to be shown as a medical necessity and approved, and that was her next goal to attain for me. It honestly didn't seem to take much. We had been talking the pros and cons of triage PT versus inpatient PT for some time, and we both felt that the Physical and Occupational Therapy I would get at Frazier would help me get back to being me faster than anything else, so she simply approved it. That's it. It was as simple as "Yes, I think that's what you need, too. So we will go ahead and approve it. Call Kentucky Prosthetics and have them get you scheduled for therapy!"

I will refrain from using names, as I am uncertain of the company's policies regarding such, but I'll certainly always remember her and everything she did for me. She was my friend, my advocate, and one of my biggest cheerleaders. Her efforts on my behalf saved me a lot of stress and heartache, and I wouldn't have recovered as much as I have without her assistance.

If you are an amputee who is fighting your insurance right now over you prosthetic care, I guarantee that you have some type of case worker or case manager assigned to you. I cannot stress enough the importance of contacting and building a relationship with that person. When you are a faceless number or name on a computer screen you are nothing more than that, a case for them to process. Get to know your case manager, you just might make a new friend, and find a sympathetic ear to help you along in your own fight to recovery. If nothing else, you might attain a better understanding of why you are being turned down, and might get advice on how to get the paperwork filled out for success. Insurance relies on codes for filing, and defining what will be covered and what is not. Sometimes an approval is nothing more than figuring out the proper codes to put on the paperwork. Your case manager can help you with that.

Even with approval, getting back into Frazier took some time. Beds weren't immediately available, and I had to have a room on the proper floor. I continued with my crawling, exercises, and walker assisted jaunts around the house while waiting for the phone to ring. Once again, I was in a holding pattern for recovery and the waiting was nearly more than I could handle. Finally, nearly a month after I had received my legs from the guy in the big brown truck, I got the call. There was a bed available and they were ready to start my therapy. I was going back to Louisville.

20 - REHAB

Although the room layouts were the same, everything seemed so very different than my first stay in the Frazier tower. Before, I had tubes and lines poking in me, and sensors and monitors stuck all over my body. This time, I had nothing. No more beep-beep-beeping all the time, no sludge flowing through a tube down my nose or throat, and best of all *no masks*. I still had nurses that would come in to take my pulse, heart rate, and blood pressure, but it seemed more like a formality than a necessity.

This time, I could go and do what I wanted as long as I didn't have physical or occupational therapy. And I had the run of the place as long as I didn't leave the grounds. I started out my stay that first evening on the right foot - so to speak - by having as much fun as possible with the staff. A nurse's aide who had never worked with me before brought me my obligatory hospital "care package" with hair brush, hand sanitizer and other assorted necessities all in a little pink tub. One of those necessities happened to be a pair of fuzzy yellow sock-footies with rubber grips on the bottom.

As the poor aide went through the tub telling me everything that was in there for me, I had to give her a deadpan look when she told me the footies would keep my feet warm and keep me from slipping. All I asked her was if she realized she was offering fuzzy slippers to a guy with no feet, and she choked up and left the room. She must have been new. How was I to know that she couldn't take a joke?

After all my walker-stepping back home I thought I was ahead of the game, and the very next morning my first therapy session would put me to the test. It was an occupational therapy session on the use of shower chairs and handicapped toilet seats, and my OT decided since I thought I could walk, we would just head on down the hall and up the elevator to the next floor up. That morning I learned the importance of pacing yourself, but I made it to our destination.

That first session would set the stage for an antagonistic relationship with one of my therapists. We spent much of our time arguing about me preferring to sit in the floor of a shower to bathe, and her belief that sitting on a plastic chair with a soapy hind-in was safer. She could not comprehend why I wouldn't want to use the chair, because that was the accepted method for persons who are wheelchair bound. Her arguments to me that day have led to one of my biggest problems with therapy in general for amputees.

When you are in a wheelchair, for whatever reason, the official therapy playbook has a set of rules that apply to everyone, be they amputees like myself, paraplegics, quadriplegics, stroke victims, etc. That entire playbook assumes that the wheelchair user has absolutely no use of their legs, and most amputees do. Putting an amputee in a box with someone who is paralyzed limits that amputee's options for movement. We may not have all of our legs, but the parts we have left work! I had already taught myself to do all my transfers without the dreaded slide board, and I could hop up onto a table or bed more than a foot taller than my chair unaided. I didn't need a slide board or a shower chair, but because I was forced into a box with all other users I was supposed to use them. Therapists need to allow some non-conformism. If things are ruled out without good reason, they could seriously limit the potential of their patients.

I would end up having more argumentative discussions with this OT over other things, but luckily my time with her was limited over the course of my stay. I quickly found that most of my time would be spent with my previous physical therapists, Mike and Emily, and with an occupational therapist named Mary Beth. It would be these three that would become my core team of therapists during my ten day stay, and they all worked my ass off.

My regime was a total of six full hours a day in therapy with thirty minute breaks in between. I spent a lot of time walking in circles with a walker in a therapy gym, and when I wasn't working my legs with either Mike or Emily I was with Mary Beth trying to make what was left of my left hand function again. I spent a lot of time with other patients playing board games, stacking blocks, and picking up odd shaped things, all with my left hand.

It had been stiff for quite some time, and I could only close my hand to about the diameter on a soda pop can. Mary Beth changed all that for me. Between her therapy sessions and some really cool treatment tricks, we got the swelling that had been a constant in my hand down to a minimum, and I could finally bend my residual digits.

On the PT side of things Emily and Mike would put me through the bars to learn how to walk on legs that felt like stilts more often than not, and I began learning to balance myself with little to no aid. I still spent plenty of time on the therapy tables doing exercises, and I was taught some stretches that would help with my wheelchair shaped lumbar area. It was on one of these tables on my second day back at Frazier when I was surprised to hear a familiar cry of " NO! NO! NO!" from another patient. I don't know if she had been there the entire time or had recently returned like I had, but there was my fellow amputee "Crybaby".

Here she was once again refusing to do what needed to be done, and I could no longer feel sorry for her, I was becoming disgusted with her. I kept thinking back to the words Mike had said to me on my first visit to Frazier when I was learning to be human again. *I can't make you go to your therapy, but if you don't... Why are you here?* That moment in the therapy room listening to Crybaby was a defining moment for me, and it would solidify an attitude that I keep to this day.

When Kentucky Prosthetics decided they would finally get out of the Stone Age and have a website done I was asked for a quote in regards to how I deal with being an amputee. It wasn't a very long quote I gave them, and one of the last things I said was the most important, because it was pounded into my very soul listening to Crybaby whine about having to stand up out of her wheelchair.

"The only limitations you have are the ones *you* put on yourself."

I can't say as I had ever seen those words smashed

together in such a way before I wrote them, but they still mean the same thing no matter how you say them.

"If you fall off the bike, get back on."

"If at first you don't succeed, try, try again."

"When someone knocks you down, come back up swinging."

"Do or do not, there is no try."

Yeah, that last one is my personal favorite. The whole point really is simple: If you're going to do something, do it. I know, that doesn't sound nearly as motivational, but then again I don't make my living as a motivational speaker. Being inspirational or motivating is really not the point of telling my story. I do hope that everyone who reads my words walks away with a better understanding of themselves and their own limits.

That's right, limits. We all have them. Only a fool would tell themselves that there are no limits in life, because there are. Finding your limits- now that is a bit harder. I could tell you many a story of idiots I have either extracted from twisted vehicles or recovered from river bottoms after a three day water rescue op who thought they had no limits. Good sense and HIPAA laws prevent me from telling these tales, but I think you get the point.

If you happen to be a new amputee reading this, don't be discouraged by my words, as that is not my intent. Let me say it a different way for you. You are the only person in your life allowed to lower your bar, while everyone else around you is only allowed to raise it. So, if you are reading this in a therapy hospital room, this means that you are allowed to tell yourself during your therapy session, "I don't think I can make those five steps back to my wheelchair."

Your therapist, on the other hand, is allowed to say "Yes, you can and you will." If you have been in therapy - ever - than you have already experienced this, if you haven't, prepare yourself. Therapists are great tormentors that way.

This also means that you can say, "Move my wheelchair back, I want to take a few more steps!" The therapist will normally oblige you. On about the second day of gait training at Frazier I was nearing the end of a walking session in the bars. I had gone down several times while using the bars hand-over-hand to keep me up and balanced, but I wanted a little taste of walking on my own. I raised my own "bar" so to speak by asking if I could try one more time, and without hands. With only a few minutes left in my session, I lined up for one more go down the bars, and this time I was determined to do it with no hands. And that is exactly what I did. I looked like a toddler doing it, but I did it. I was so excited and so tired when I made it to the end of the bars that I thought I must be passing out. I was hearing a roaring in my ears that I assumed meant I had over-stepped my limits and was about to hit the floor from exhaustion.

Nope.

That roaring in my ears turned out to be a crowd of other therapy patients as well as their PT's and PTA's cheering and clapping for me. As I slid down into the sweet bliss of my wheelchair one of the physical therapists leaned down and whispered to me, "You inspired a lot of people today doing that." I am not often humbled as it just isn't in my nature, but that day I was. I had determined that walking unaided was within my limits, and for the first time since I was admitted into ICU I had walked on my own. In the process I had given my fellow therapy patients something that they could hope for, a reason to raise their own bar.

I am sure I would have come to that attitude eventually, but the day I laid on the therapy table listening to Crybaby whine about her single amputation made me want to test every limit I had. I did not want to be a whiner, I did not want to be a crybaby, and I did not *ever* want to be a bad example of a peer to other amputees.

During my ten or so days at gait training I learned to walk with forearm crutches, I learned how to navigate stairs, and I learned how to walk up slopes. I was not nearly strong enough yet to do any of those things without walking aids, but I was assured by my therapists that strength would come with practice and time. My evenings were free, and I could do mostly what I wanted. I spent a lot of time wheeling around the halls and exploring areas of the hospital complex, revisiting areas that I had been in before and saying hello to former caregivers from other floors. It seemed so important to me to track them down and thank them for how patient they had been with me, and to thank them for their kindness to my family.

The weekend that I spent during my stay included only half-days of therapy, and I was allowed visitors. I didn't have any family members staying with me this time around so I did get a bit lonely for conversation that didn't involve someone telling me to take a pain med, or to do four more reps of exercises. I went to my therapy sessions that Saturday with my buddy

Matthew who had driven in from Lexington to hang out for the day. We had spent so much of our friendship pushing ourselves to the limit on the mountain bike trails that it seemed very natural for him to be there to push me to my limits during therapy.

He stayed and ate lunch with me down in the cafeteria, and we spent the rest of the afternoon hanging outside in the sunshine. It was that day hanging out with my old friend that made me realize that I was no longer so afraid to be seen by other people, I no longer felt like I was such a freak. I may have been in a wheelchair, but I had my prosthesis on and I was feeling *whole* again. I could look strangers in the eye and I didn't feel ashamed of the fact that they always had to look at my legs before they looked me in the face. It was a very liberating feeling.

Part of my physical therapy with Mike was spent in that very same area outside. We would ride the elevator down to the ground floor with me in my wheelchair, and as soon as we made it out to the sidewalk I would be out and walking with crutches. Walking up and down those gentle slopes was a major task, but it didn't feel nearly as clinical as my workouts in the therapy room. The simple act of sitting down on a sidewalk bench when I grew tired was one more thing to count as being normal, and the sun shining on my face was therapy in itself.

If I wasn't being put to the task of walking and strength train with Mike, Emily, or any of the other PT's and PTA's that comprised their team, I was re-learning normal life skills with Mary Beth. Normal life skills are the staples of Occupational Therapy, and they are very important. It is a true shame that OT doesn't receive nearly enough attention when it comes to therapy, because it is very important. I or anyone else in my situation can build strength and learn to walk on prosthetics with physical therapy and can be considered a success, but if we try to brush our teeth with a comb we are still not ready for real life yet. That is what OT is for, the little life skills we take for granted.

Mary Beth worked with me on my hand, of course, but she also helped me figure out how to get plates down out of cabinets while supporting myself with crutches, how to use a can opener again, and how to do rudimentary cooking tasks. She even made me bake cookies. They were chocolate chip, and they were tasty - if I do say so myself.

My progress and good attitude had not gone unnoticed by the medical and therapy staff. Not long before my last day at Frazier the head of therapy, Dr. Williamson, came to me and asked me to share my story with a new amputee. My experience so far with peers had been deplorable, and I was determined to make a better impression on this new amputee than Crybaby and others had made on me. The gentleman I was asked to meet was on a recovery floor above me where he was recuperating from losing a single leg below the knee. The day I went to introduce myself both he and his wife were there, and I talked about the progress I had made and handed him one of my legs so he could get a feel for what he was in for. I am told that my visit improved this couple's outlook on his recovery considerably, and the last update I received was that he is back to jogging at least two miles a day.

I wasn't even yet out of my own therapy and I had

my first session as a peer counselor. That one visit was a defining moment for me, and I knew then that I wanted to spend as much of my time as possible helping new amputees cope with their limb loss. I didn't want *any* amputee to have to experience the attitude of defeat I had found in my first peer encounters.

It was my entire therapy team's efforts that got me prepared for both walking and living life again, and they all worked me hard during my time there. I had gained so much of myself back again going through that intensive therapy at Frazier, and by the time I left on my last day I felt I was ready to take on the world. My mother and my brother Wes came to pick me up, I said goodbye to my wonderful care and therapy staff, and we headed for home.

Along the way we stopped in Evansville to say hello to Jenny and Rayetta at my old office, and then we stopped in at one of my favorite restaurants for sushi. I was walking with forearm crutches the entire time, and I was feeling very proud of myself. I really overdid it that day and forgot my limits, and when we finally made it home that evening I knew I would be paying the price for it.

As I took my prosthesis and liners off while sitting in my chair I did the daily skin check that every amputee learns to do early on, and I found and angry looking red spot on the bottom of my left leg. It looked like an acne spot with a black center, and the skin around it was inflamed. I knew what it was immediately, and I was not happy. I hadn't had a Behcet's flair up in months, and now when I was ready to walk it had reared its ugly head.

21 - STANDING TOUGH

It only took me a few days of trying to walk with a BD ulcer to realize that I was doing nothing but making it worse. The pressure I was exerting on the ends of my limbs in the sockets was exacerbating the wound at a tremendous rate, and the pimple-sized ulcer quickly grew into a monster the size of a quarter. I had spent all that time in gait training building strength, skill, and balance, and I was going to have to take the legs off and keep them off. I was crushed.

Day after day I began the laborious and familiar task of wound care and bandage changing. I had learned many tricks over the years to contain the growth of skin ulcers related to BD and I was employing every one of them in my arsenal. I had to stay on my rear all the time and I kept the ends of my limbs elevated and above my heart. When your immune system attacks your own body it utilizes swelling to ramp up its attack, and keeping swelling out of a symptomatic area can make all the difference in recovery time. Just as someone with swollen and tender joints might apply ice or heat to control blood flow and manage the lymphatic system's attempts to cushion an area, I had to do the same to keep inflammation out of my limbs.

There are quite a few prescribed medications for

auto-immune sufferers, from pain medications to heavy-duty steroids. I had spent much of my time while in the hospital on pain drugs and narcotics, and when I came home I swore off the use of any prescription pain killers. I have a high tolerance for pain, and I did not want to become dependent on pills for pain so I used simple over-the-counter pain relievers such as acetaminophen and ibuprofen to control both swelling and pain. I have seen too many people become pill junkies, and I was not going to become one.

I couldn't have afforded prescription pain medications even if I had wanted them, as my time on short term disability had finally played out, and my company had been forced to terminate my employment. That was an odd thing for me, being officially unemployed. I have never been without a job. Not since I had moved out on my own at eighteen. I had been gainfully employed for twenty years, and had never left one job without having another one already lined up. No job meant no insurance, no income. Dire straits for me. I had applied for Social Security disability benefits and been told I was approved, but I had no idea when payments would start and medical coverage had a mandatory two year wait.

My prosthetic legs and fingers had been covered, as well as some of my hospital stay and therapy, but I had mounds and mounds of individual medical bills I still had to pay. I had no insurance, no income, mounting bills and a Behcet's wound keeping me from getting on my new legs. Things were beginning to look very bleak for me. I didn't qualify for any state aid even though I was unable to work and had lost multiple limbs. That system is simply not set up to help people in my situation. I was the wrong gender and didn't have enough children to qualify for housing assistance or Medicaid, and any other government assistance programs totally failed me.

My friends and family didn't fail me, though. They had a plan to keep me afloat, and with the help of our VFW post they were going to keep me from going under.

Everyone pitched in to help and plan, and in April of 2011 a huge fundraising event was planned for me. It was an amazing and unforgettable event, as all of the friends in my life are somewhat separated. My friends from out of town that I have known for so long had never met any of my friends from back home, and that night nearly everyone I cared about from near and far was all there to help support my cause. Tons of donations were made for an auction, piles and piles of food were prepared to sell in plates, and a karaoke dance was held afterward. For the first time since I had been in the hospital I had the chance to sing a few songs with good friends, have a few drinks, and just hang out like a normal person.

I was still suffering from the BD wound on my leg and was in a wheelchair, but I had put my legs on for the occasion. I couldn't walk for fear of causing myself damage, but I did stand up and take the microphone to thank everyone for coming out to support me. That was the first time most of those friends and family had seen me stand on my prosthetic legs, and they were ecstatic to see me standing tall once again. I was pretty happy myself. The generosity of all those people helped keep me afloat until Social Security came through for me, and I began to have a bit of breathing room.

By the first part of May my leg was nearly healed, and I was certain that I would soon be able to put my legs back on and start walking. I have always tried to minimize how much I tell to my family about the effects of Behcet's, and I followed that routine with this small bout as well. I told them only that I had an ulcer that prevented me from using my new prosthesis, and that it was slowly healing. It had gotten pretty bad, and I didn't want them to worry too much, so I kept them somewhat in the dark. That would prove to be a mistake.

My parents had such high hopes after I had come home from therapy and gait training, and seeing me stay in my wheel chair or sitting with my legs constantly propped up was wearing on them. I assumed they understood that it would be a bad thing for me to walk until the ulcer was completely healed, and I was wrong in that assumption. My father had all he could stand of seeing his son sitting down, and he decided to take measures into his own hands.

We have around five acres on our property, and dad has a tractor he uses to work the land and mow the yard. One afternoon I sat in my room listening to dad running around the yard on his machine, having no idea what he was doing. His plans soon became readily apparent when he appeared at the door of my room and told me, "Put your legs on. I'm your physical therapist now." the one person in the world I have a hard time talking back to is my old man, and instead of telling him me walking would be a really bad thing I hung my head and started the long process of pulling on my liners and ply-socks and putting on my legs.

Down in the back yard by a small yard-barn my father had set up several posts and his tractor bucket with ropes strung about them. My dad had decided I had had enough of sitting around, and had set up therapy walking "bars" made of ropes. With the help of my son I was made to climb onto a riding lawnmower and then ride down to my father's impromptu therapy room. My father stood by as I was forced to try to walk back and forth between those two ropes on rough and uneven ground, and he would not allow me to stop until he thought I had worked at it enough.

With every unbalanced and inept step on that rough ground I felt the Behcet's wound on my leg becoming more and more painful. I couldn't tell my old man this was a bad idea, because he seemed to have it in his that mind my refusal to use my legs to walk was based on laziness. My father thought I had given up, and he had no idea my wound had been as bad as it was.

I spent one entire afternoon down in the back yard fumbling along in between those ropes, all the while cringing at the pain at the end of my leg that was getting worse with every step. When my father decided I had worked hard enough, I was allowed to go back up to the house and take my legs off. I didn't want to. I was afraid of what I would find at the end of my left leg. By the time I made it back to my room my mother had come home from work, so she was in the house when I finally removed my prosthesis.

I knew it was going to be bad when I saw red spread throughout the bottom of my liner. As I rolled that thick polyurethane covering off my leg blood began to drip onto the floor. The 2x2 gauze pad I had covered my wound in was soaked completely through with blood and vitriol, and I was frightened with what I would find when I removed it. That morning my ulcer had been the size of a piece of rice and nearly scabbed over. Another week and it would have been completely healed. When I pulled off the blood-soaked gauze, I found my nearly healed ulcer was now a wound the size of a silver dollar. In those few hours of "therapy" my immune system - aided by Behcet's - had found the ulcer and eaten away a two square inch spot of flesh.

The entire house heard my bellow of anguish, and my mother was the first to make it to my side. She needed no words from me because she saw the ruin of my leg, but I gave her words anyway. "Look at it! Now it's never going to heal!" After that I could no longer speak. Sobs were wracking my body so hard I could barely breathe.

That is how I was when my father made it to my room, standing in the door and harshly asking, "What? What's wrong?" My mother looked at him then pointed at my now-huge skin ulcer, not saying a word. My dad took one look at my leg and then turned and rushed out. I didn't speak to my father for a long time after that. I was upset with him for making me walk and I was upset with myself for not standing up and saying no. I had planned on walking by Memorial Day, and instead I spent that holiday in my room listening to the lovely sound of loud motorcycle pipes as they rode passed the house down on the street. My own motorcycle not a hundred yards from me in storage and I had yet to even see it. I cried that day in front of my entire family, and they thought I was falling into depression. They had no idea that those tears weren't from sadness, those were tears of anger. I was madder than hell that I couldn't walk, couldn't drive, couldn't ride my motorcycle, and they just couldn't understand.

I would spend the next two months waiting for that aggravated wound to heal. I was beginning to feel like all my hard work during therapy had gone to waste, every day without walking my body atrophied more and more. I continued to crawl and keep up with my leg exercises, but those pale in comparison to actually walking every day. Boredom was once again my constant companion and I spent much of that time blogging, reading, and gaming.

I had discovered an entire online world in a multiplayer online role playing game, and I spent countless nights meeting new friends and hanging out in a virtual world. I had never had much patience for that type of game before, but with a forced sit-down while my leg tried to heal again I was looking for anything to relieve boredom. An MMORPG provided me the opportunity to game, talk to friends, and go to cool places without ever getting out of the house or the wheelchair. If you ever happen to find yourself in an extended bed-rest situation, this type of game will keep you occupied and surprisingly sane.

I eventually joined a "guild" (a large group of players who are essentially on the same "team") and made many new friends. As I continued to play during those months of forced immobility I found that I had gained a certain amount of notoriety. I had never been afraid to talk about my circumstances or my amputations to my guild mates and in-game friends, and they in turn began to tell others about me. I was overwhelmed by the amount of respect I received from complete strangers of all ages, and I would constantly get private messages from people who told me they had read my blog and that I inspired them. The kindness and outpouring of support I encountered while playing a simple game really helped me get through those months of downtime, and I made friendships that continue to this day with great people I met playing a silly game.

It would take me four months to fully heal that ulcer, and by August of 2011 I began the process of learning to walk all over again. My balance was completely gone, as well as most of my leg strength. But I still remembered all the exercises that Mike and Emily had put me through and I started back over at square one. Besides the simple fact that I wanted to walk and was tired of being immobile, I had other motivators for getting on my feet again. An old friend from my days as a corporate axe-man had called to catch up with me, and she wanted me to come celebrate her birthday with her.

I had never had much luck making friends with regular employees, but my friend Krystal had never known me at a branch level. We had worked together as corporate employees on and off since my Indianapolis days, and whenever we happened to be visiting the same branch office we would make it a point to hang out. She had eventually left the company and moved to Texas with her fiancée, but we had always made it a point to keep in touch. Her birthday was coming up, and she had a long trip planned to drive through the Southwestern portion of the United States while stopping along the way and camping. She wanted me to go, and I wasn't turning her down. I needed to get to walking!

I had to start back out with a walker, but progressed quickly back into forearm crutches. One of the first things I did when I was able to get outside with my crutches and walk was go visit both my motorcycle and truck. My truck had been in Nashville for months, and my brother Kyle had brought it up earlier in the spring. I wasn't yet able to trust myself on my own outside, so my son spent a lot of time escorting me where I wanted to go. The truck was parked no more than sixty or so yards away down a slope, but I might as well have been climbing down a mountain getting to it.

I had been told during rehab that I would no longer be able to drive a manual transmission vehicle, and my little four-wheel-drive was a stick. I had asked on plenty of amputee forums about driving a stick with two prosthetic legs, and found that there were many amputees like me who still used a manual transmission. That was all I needed to hear. My son and I would daily make a trip down the hill to my truck, and he would climb in the cab with me while I drove around the yard. I hadn't been behind the wheel of an automobile in eight months, and looking out the windshield of that old truck while puttering around the yard was like looking at freedom. My family had already let it be known that I would be driving a stick shift over their dead bodies so I knew I would eventually have to sell that truck and get an automatic, but for the time being I was enjoying proving wrong every person who told me it couldn't be done.

My motorcycle, on the other hand, was a different story. My old Suzuki was a tall bike, with a relatively high center of gravity. Several times during our trips down that hill my son and I would go check on my bike where it sat in storage in a little shell of a house. Having prosthetic legs means having fairly immobile ankles and less range of motion in the knees, I can't bend my knees past a ninety degree angle while wearing my prosthesis. This limited range of motion made it far too difficult to get my leg over my bike, and when I could get seated on it I couldn't keep my feet totally flat on the ground. I couldn't hold proper balance on my bike, and I couldn't get my feet to stay on the pegs. They were mounted too far back past my limited range of motion. I wouldn't be able to ride my beloved bike, at least not for quite some time.

Knowing my family's thoughts on my driving, I searched for and found a new truck to buy that I hoped they would not complain so much about. It was the same make and model as my old four-by-four, but with an extended cab and an automatic transmission. The gentleman I bought it from was kind enough to bring it to me to look at first, and I purchased it the very same day. The whole point of getting an automatic was to appease everyone else so I could drive, so I was crestfallen when my father told me, "You can look at it and sit in it all you want, but I better not see it on the road."

I was having none of that.

I realized fully well that my family had just gone through hell watching me nearly die and then losing my legs, but I had had quite enough of being treated as if I were a child. I had been stuck in their house for months, only able to leave when I could talk someone into coming and getting me, dealing with packing up my wheelchair into the trunk and chauffeuring me around where I needed to go. I was becoming very weary of relying on others, and I was ready for a little independence.

I found that independence in a set of automotive hand controls. If everyone's problem seemed to stem from driving with my prosthetic feet on the pedals, than I would give in and get a set of hand controls so no one could gripe about me driving. It took no time at all for me to find and purchase a set of portable controls online, and when they arrived they were even simpler to install and use. The controls were a set of steel rods with handles on one end and clamps on the other. One clamp connected to the gas pedal, and the other to the brake. A strap held them at hand level for me, and easy as that I was driving again.

I had planned on taking a few rounds across the yard to get a feel for the brake and gas, but was surprised to find the controls automatically felt familiar in my hand. I had been riding motorcycles for years, and using hand controls in a truck is not unlike twisting a bike throttle and pulling the brake lever. That very first time I didn't even have my legs on, so I broke down my wheelchair and packed it into the passenger seat and I was on the road.

Being able to drive again put me one step closer to freedom, and I spent more than an hour just cruising around the highways and back roads outside of town enjoying being independent of the need for help getting away from the house. I was well aware of the fact that I would eventually be seen, and as it always is in a small town nothing stays secret for long. So I knew I had to deal with my parents head-on about my driving. They both happened to be at work and it was close to lunchtime, so I decided to make a trip through a drive-thru and pick them up some lunch. That seemed like a perfectly good excuse for dropping by the salon, and being as the salon was a public place, I assumed that any freaking out on their part would be kept to a minimum.

So, with a sack of burgers and fries on the seat beside me I pulled up directly in front of the salon and honked, then waited for all hell to break loose. It was my father who recognized my new truck first, and I could see his look of astonishment and disbelief as he left his client sitting in his chair and made a bee-line for the door. I could tell from the look on my father's face as he stepped through the door that I was about to get a royal ass-chewing. I had seen that face every time I had gotten in trouble since I was a little boy. I knew it well.

Before he had a chance to say a word I opened my door to reveal the newly installed hand controls. As I gestured at the controls with one hand and handed him the bag of food with the other I said, "Look, I got hand controls. Thought I would bring you guys some lunch!"

Never in my life had I seen my old man speechless, but just for a moment as he stared at those controls he had nothing to say. The look on his face went from anger to total acceptance, and all he had to ask was how well they worked. I told him they worked just fine, and that was it. I never heard another cross word about me getting behind the wheel, and when I drove away from the salon that day I had my independence back. I no longer had to ask to be taken anywhere, I could go where I wanted, and more importantly I could now go by myself to pick up my son, something I had not done since I had been admitted into the hospital the previous September.

Every day I got a little stronger, and every day I pushed myself a little harder. I had a September deadline for a road trip, and I was not going to miss it! Being able to drive meant I could get out of the house and go again, and naturally I gravitated towards the fire department. Walking into that truck bay under my own power was a glorious feeling, even if I still had to use crutches. Everyone was glad to see me, and no one cut me any breaks, which was exactly what I needed. Getting trash talked by the men I had once fought fires with showed me that they didn't pity me or feel sorry for me. To them I was the same old me.

On one of my visits down to the station I was taken by surprise when Brad Curry, now chief Brad Curry, asked me to come have a sit down with him in his office. I could no longer fight a fire or make an ambulance run, but it seems that Brad thought all the time I had put in was still valuable jab experience, and he asked me how I felt about coming on part time as a dispatcher. I was barely back to driving and walking and I had been offered a job.

I was going back to work at the fire department.

I told Brad the same thing I have always said, I just want to help, so if they needed someone to help dispatch, I would do it. Dispatch wasn't anything close to making ambulance runs or working a fire ground, but it was a chance for me to get back to a place that I dearly love, working around old friends and feeling like a productive member of society again.

September finally rolled around, and although I was still on crutches I was going on my trip to see Krystal. Our plan was for me to drive to Dallas, load up all of her camping gear, meet some friends who would be coming along, and head for the Rocky Mountains in Colorado. We were then going to make our way out to Utah to visit an animal rescue sanctuary, as one of Krystal's passions in life is helping animals. It was a tall order, and I was worried that the trip would be too much for me, but I went anyway.

With the help of my dad and my son I packed my truck, and I made off for the drive to Dallas. I had spent so much of my life driving for work that the drive down was both simple and enjoyable. I have always been one to prefer to start long drives in the evening, and so late one night I left the house in my packed truck and drove straight through to Dallas, arriving early the next day. Getting to see my dear friend after such a long time and after everything I had been through was wonderful, and finding the courage to make the drive by myself when I could barely walk made me feel like I could conquer anything.

After an evening of catching up we got her gear loaded with the help of her fiancée, and the next morning we were off for our trip to the mountains. After we met up with the rest of her friends we drove up through Texas and into New Mexico, finally stopping for the night in a state park in Colorado. That night it rained buckets on us, and we all spent a cold evening huddled under a tarp tied off to the camper shell of my truck. The rain finally slacked off enough for tents to be set up, and I think all of us were glad to get to pack up and move on the next morning!

Our final destination in Colorado was high up in the mountains, and after what seemed like hours of driving on rutted gravel roads we finally came to our planned camping site. It was a small open field surrounded by tall fir trees, and we had a majestic view overlooking the valley below us. Here I was, not quite a year since I had nearly died, and I was standing in a meadow in the Rockies on prosthetics legs I had yet to master. It was an incredible feeling knowing I had cheated death, and my reward for living was getting to make this trip. The terrain was tough for me as I was still on crutches, but Krystal was there to help me out and take care of me.

The same rain and cold that we had met on our first night followed us up the mountain, and we were only there a few days when it was decided that the weather was just too bad for us to enjoy ourselves. Outwardly I was disappointed like everyone else, but inside I was relieved. I had experienced something very new to me during that short stay on the mountain, and it would be a dark cloud that would shadow me for the rest of the trip.

When I was on flat and level ground I could get around fairly easily. As long as I had my forearm crutches I had no problems doing whatever I needed to do or go where I needed to go. Up on the mountain there was no flat ground, and trying to get around in that mountain meadow was nearly too much for me. I found myself spending a lot of time sitting down because it was all I could do, and much like being in a wheelchair I felt trapped. That made me irritable and cranky, and brought on the totally new experience of pure panic. Only recently have I recognized that I was having a major anxiety attack up on that mountain, brought on by a simple feeling of helplessness. I didn't stop feeling helpless until we packed up and came back down, finally being chased off by the bad weather.

The entire birthday trip for Krystal didn't end so badly, despite the weather. We made it back to Dallas a few days later, and she was able to get a flight out to Utah to volunteer at the animal sanctuary. There was no way with the weather moving in that we could have continued on with our plans to camp and drive. And I bowed out at even the thought of flying. I was not ready to tackle an airport in prosthetics. The rain had made us all a bit miserable, but it was worth it to see such a good friend again. I didn't see a drop of rain on the drive back to Kentucky.

During all of my downtime earlier that year, I had plenty of time to think about what I wanted to do with the rest of my life. Before I had fallen ill I'd planned on nursing school, but after all my time lying in a hospital bed nursing just didn't appeal to me as much. I had decided while still in therapy that I wanted to help other amputees, and I decided that physical therapy might be the best way to facilitate that goal. What better way to help other amputees and be a positive role model and peer than to be someone who literally helps them get back on their feet?

As soon as I got back from the camping trip I began to focus on my goal. I wanted to become a physical therapy assistant to help my fellow amputees. Being able to attend college meant getting away from the crutches and walking without aids, and doing so quickly. I decided that I might be able to get some help and advice to get away from crutches if I joined a support group, so I began looking around in my area. I didn't find any.

The closest support group I could find ended up being in Paducah, Kentucky, over an hour away from me. I got into contact with the group leader, Terri Ross, and she convinced me to make the trip over. I had been working very hard at building my strength and balance, and by the time I made it to my first meeting of Paducah Area Amputees in Action in late October I was down to using a single forearm crutch. That first meeting was a true eye opener for me. For once I wasn't in a minority. Everyone there had experienced limb loss. I was the only bilateral lower limb amputee, and the only amputee with upper extremity loss, but it made no difference. I was with a group of people who had the same struggles as I had, and they were continuing to live their lives.

I also learned at that first meeting that I was somewhat of an anomaly. I very rarely complain to anyone about problems I encounter as an amputee, and even when I am feeling awful I do my best to put on a grin and push through. My progress and my attitude seemed to be a surprise to the group, and their praise made me want to work even harder to get back to normal and to throw my crutches away! I walked away from that first group meeting feeling like I had just made a difference in peoples' lives, and I had made some new friends in the process.

I continued working at the fire department on dispatch, and spending every moment I could on my feet, walking to build my balance and strength. I walked so much that I shrunk myself out of my sockets. I had been told by my prosthetist, Matt, that the more I walked, the more my limbs would shrink in a process that could take several years. In less than three short months of consistent hard work and walking, I shrunk my distal ends to the point that my prosthetic sockets were too big to walk in.

I made a trip back to Louisville to Kentucky Prosthetics for a new casting session for a new set of sockets. With my first trip back to college in nearly twenty years just over the horizon, a snug fitting pair of sockets was going to be essential. I think everyone was surprised at my progress, because when I walked in that day in early November I was using nothing more than a cane. I had been on my legs for only two and a half months and was able to walk unaided for short periods of time, and used the cane only for extended walks. I was quickly turning into a success story.

By the end of November I had walked into my second support group meeting, and this time without any walking aids whatsoever. My crutches were stored away in a closet and I had begun leaving my cane behind the seat of my truck. I just didn't need it anymore. All my hard work had paid off and I was living my life again, my way, and on my terms.

Another milestone occurred near the end of that month. My son Tyler turned sixteen years old and got his driving permit. He was growing up, and I was very glad to still be around to see it happen. It had only been a year since I had lay in that hospital bed looking down at my newly amputated legs and fingers wondering how I was ever going to live any kind of life, but I had made it through it all. I was back on my feet and walking, and I planned on the coming year to be much better than the previous!

The month of December just flew by with preparations for my upcoming semester of college, Christmas, and family gatherings. Before I knew it the New Year was upon us, and the first week of January 2012, I walked onto campus and sat down in a classroom. I had become a college student with a firm goal of walking out as a PTA.

22 - NO DOUBTS, NO EXCUSES

Returning to college meant returning to a regular routine, something I sorely needed. Having spent so much of my adult life working, down time with nothing to do didn't sit very well. I was able to look at college as if it were a full time job with schedules, projects, deadlines, and supervisors to report to. Most of my fellow students were fresh-faced children just out of high school, and suddenly I found myself being the old guy with a much different work ethic than those around me.

I had problems with few classes, and most of my teachers and professors were excellent educators. They were understanding of some of my limitations in regards to how I completed my work. My handwriting before I lost my limbs was atrocious, and I think losing the fingers from my left hand might have actually improved my scrawl somewhat. As much as I had tried, I still found my right hand useless except for the most menial tasks so I still used my left for as much as I could. I had gotten my sought-after X-Fingers and they were an amazing advancement in technology, but they were so delicate that I couldn't use them for ordinary everyday tasks.

This wasn't a limitation of the prosthetics, but more of a problem with the configuration of my amputations. Most users on the X-Fingers have single digit losses, and I was missing all - or parts of all- of my fingers. I had practically nothing left, so even with state-of-the-art prosthetic fingers, I had no strength to do simple things like carry a book bag or pull open heavy doors. And I did not have quite enough dexterity to hold a pen or pencil while wearing them so most days on campus I left them at home.

When you don't have fingernails where your fingers end, every little bump and jar is painful, so I devised a much sturdier but much less dexterous set of fingers I could utilize for everyday use. They started merely as metal rods stuffed inside of a glove, but have now evolved into much more. My glove prosthesis allowed me to grasp door handles with strength, pick up heavy objects, and keep my sensitive partial digits protected from my own clumsiness. It was far too stiff and bulky for the delicate task of writing, so I would doff it while in the classroom and write with a bare left hand.

My experiences with prosthetic fingers taught me an invaluable lesson that all amputees eventually learn. There is no one single apparatus that will allow you to do whatever you want to do. You cannot sprint on a foot made for walking, and a foot made for running is difficult to walk in. There simply is no one perfect device for all things, so we as amputees learn to do different things with different prosthesis and adapt.

When I wasn't on campus I was still working dispatch at the department and writing on my blog, and I was surprised to discover I was building a readership. I had done something with my blog that had rarely been accomplished by others. I had blogged everything from the beginning of my ordeal.

My blog was suddenly being used as a resource by doctors, physical and occupational therapists, and even my own prosthetics team. As they would encounter new amputees they would tell them my story, about my progress, and about my chronicling it all while it was happening, and would then send those new amputees to go read my blog.

I had yet to make it through my first semester of college and I was already helping new amputees and being asked to participate in events geared towards the care and therapy of my peers. My words and my website were being used by therapy educators as a teaching tool in college classrooms and I was making presentations to first year OT students, sharing my struggles and triumphs and impressing on them my views on different kinds of thinking when it comes to dealing with amputees. I was invited to attend and participate at continuing education conferences for OT's and PT's; assisting with education and explaining my prosthetics at the very therapy institute that had gotten me back on my feet. I found myself in the company of Paralympic medalists, prosthetic industry professionals, and fellow amputees like myself that had made extraordinary progress. My care team from Kentucky Prosthetics was with me every step of the way, and helped me gain many new contacts that would lead to great things for me.

Local therapy clinics began contacting me, asking for help counseling patients with peer visits, and I was receiving requests via social media sites for peer visits. I learned there were many amputees in my area, and not nearly enough support for them. I did my utmost to help everyone who needed my help, and I did my best to bring new amputees with me to the support group meetings in Paducah.

The sudden attention I was receiving caused me to take a long and hard look at the progress I had made. Walking unassisted, returning to college, and sitting in the dispatch office at the station was all well and good, but it wasn't enough. I had not forgotten Matt Hayden's promise of 98%, and I had already returned to several of the basic activities I enjoyed before I lost my limbs. I realized more and more that it wasn't the 98% that concerned me, but that last two percent - the things I would never be able to do again. I began to make a list of the most important things that I wanted to once again do, almost like a bucket list. Calling these things a "bucket list" seemed so inappropriate, as they were not things I wanted to do before I kicked the "bucket." No, these were things I had once done in my life, and wanted to do again, and so my *socket list* was born.

On this list I put the most important and controversial things, things I had been told I could never do again. One of them I had already accomplished while still on crutches - driving a stick shift. That one had been easy. What would fall between the two percent? I wasn't yet sure, but I did have my list.

First and foremost was to get back on a fire engine and work a fire ground again, and along with that make ambulance runs. While I was in the coma my EMT license had come up for renewal, and as my paperwork hadn't been sent in my card had expired, so add getting my license back to the list. The very next thing to get thrown into the socket was rappelling, I wanted to climb a training tower in my harness and go over the side of a wall again. I had a need to feel the wind in my hair and a twisting throttle in my hand, so add riding a motorcycle to list, one with only two wheels, not three. The final of the most important things on my socket list would be to get once again on the Jiu Jitsu mat and train in the art I loved. I had my third belt and was working toward the fourth when work had originally pulled me away from a regular training schedule.

There would be less important goals to put on my list of things to do again while standing in my sockets, but these were the ones I was truly concerned with. I made it my goal to find out on which side of the percent sign these things would fall, so in between peer visits, college classes, dispatch, and amputee events I made my plans and did my research.

I was already sure that I would not be able to ride my own motorcycle, so I made plans to sell it and began a search for a ride I could hold up. It would be a tall order due to budget constraints, and I knew any modifications I would make to allow me to ride I would have to accomplish on my own. It took me until the middle of April, 2012, but I found the bike I needed, and the owner happened to be a friend and co-worker at the fire department.

William had been with the department for several years before I had ever even joined as a volunteer, and had risen to the rank of assistant chief. He happened to have a bike small enough for me to handle and was looking to sell it to buy himself something a bit bigger. Since my 'Zuki had yet to sell, we discussed making a deal on a trade and we decided to have a look at each other's motorcycles.

My bike hadn't been started since September of 2010 when I went into the hospital, and it had been sitting in unheated storage for just as long. I hadn't done anything with it since my son and I had gone down to look at it and I had realized I wouldn't be able to ride it, so I had my doubts as to whether or not it would even start. To my surprise with a new battery install and fresh gasoline in the tank my loud old beast of a muscle bike sprang right to life. William was most certainly interested in it after hearing the motor run, and all that was left to do was see if I could get on his bike.

Standing over that little black machine for the first time was a scary experience. It was an automatic, so it had a much lower pass-over clearance for me to swing my leg over and through, but I still didn't know if I would even be able to hold the thing up. With William and his wife Melinda standing by, I got myself onto that bike and rode for the first time since I lost my legs. I was awfully shaky starting out, but had no problems once I got rolling. It had foot rests far enough forward that I had no problems keeping my legs in place, and without the need to shift gears all I had to do was twist and go.

And go I did. I had planned on only being gone a few minutes - just long enough to see if I could keep my balance, but once I had the wind in my face I couldn't stop riding. I was doing it, I was riding again. I was on two wheels again, and it was a glorious feeling. By the time I finally returned, Melinda was so concerned that I had ridden off into a ditch that she sent William out to look for me in his truck. I was glad that the both of them hadn't gone to look for me, as I soon discovered that while I could hold it up and ride it, I couldn't reach the kickstand with my prosthetic feet! With Melinda's help I got the stand down and off the bike.

I was sad to see my GS go, as I had spent so much time customizing it and tuning the motor, but I knew it would be going to a good home and I now had a new bike to work on. It would take me some time to get the new ride road worthy, adjusted, and modified to allow me to safely gas, brake, and park it. I found with my prosthetic glove I could pull a brake lever again, and after finding all the right components to suit my needs I was back in the saddle and riding. I wasn't taking hairpin turns at 80 MPH anymore, but I was on two wheels doing what I loved. I had been told it couldn't be done and I had done it in spite - riding a motorcycle again could be marked off of my socket list.

The cold spring turned to early summer and by June I had completed my first semester of college with a 3.3 GPA, and I was riding nearly every day. Between my college homework and issues with Social Security I had to cut back my time at the station to a limited volunteer basis, but considering the summer I had in store that was for the best.

William's wife Melinda had a dear friend she had spoken to me about on numerous occasions who had amputations surprisingly similar to my own, and Melinda wanted me to give the young lady a hand. I had begun peer visits with her during the winter, and after much coaxing on my part and hard work on hers, she was finally ready to take the step toward walking again. When I had been in the hospital I had heard bits and pieces about a girl who was one floor above me at RMC that had lost her legs and fingers due to complications from an ATV accident, and my family had made every effort to keep the fact that there was an amputee in the hospital from me. We had still kept hopes of saving my legs before my first trip to Louisville, and everyone was concerned that seeing someone who had already lost their limbs might push me over the edge.

One short year later, I would find myself peer counseling that very same young lady when Melinda asked me to talk to her amputee friend Sara Jo. Perhaps "ask" is too delicate a word, as Melinda is known for neither subtlety nor delicacy - she is like a short little force of nature and there was simply no way to tell her "no." So I met with Sara Jo, and did my best to help her toward her road to recovery. I introduced her to Terri Ross and all the other great people at Paducah Area Amputees in Action, and with Terri's help we pushed Sara Jo towards success.

Somewhere along the way of my blog writing I had coined for myself a personal mantra, and for me it was both profound yet surprisingly simple. I had taken everything that had happened to me and all my plans to fight back against my circumstances and was living my life according to those ten simple words.

Survive. Live. Walk. Run. Climb. Succeed. No Doubts. No Excuses.

Every day I strived to do all those things without doubts and without excuses for failure, and it was that attitude I tried to impress on every amputee I came into contact with. Sara Jo had lost her legs a month before me, and she was still sitting in a wheelchair, trapped in her own home. The very first night we met I put her in my truck and took her to an empty parking lot to drive. Many of her family and friends had convinced her that such things would no longer be possible for her, and it was my goal to show her that she could.

It only took that one time driving around that parking lot to realize that she was not as helpless as she thought, and she immediately began testing her own limits with everything. I had learned all too well from my own experiences that having the ability to get out of the house by yourself and drive was a huge catalyst for independence, and I had just shown Sara a taste of freedom.

I had long since replaced my portable hand controls with a more permanent setup, which allowed other people to drive my truck without clamps being in the way. I had taught my own son to drive in that truck and he would not have been able to drive it with the portable set. New hand controls in my truck left my old ones gathering dust in the garage, so I gifted them to Sara Jo to use when she found a new vehicle that she could easily get into and out of.

With a little nudge in the right direction she had found her independence again, and with it a newfound desire to walk. Her circumstances had been so much different than my own, and she had not received the therapy she needed nor a proper set of prosthetic legs to walk in. She had been given an initial set of test sockets with basic feet to get started with, but an unfortunate misappropriation of funds by a former loved one had left her penniless and without insurance to continue her care. Sara Jo had the desire to walk again, but she did not have the funds.

With careful planning and a lot of help from a multitude of great people we organized a fundraiser and poker run event to help Sara Jo get started on her road to recovery. The event was planned for mid-July, and I found myself suddenly pressed for time. I had been invited to attend a class at Northwestern University in Chicago to be a test subject for a new type of prosthetic socket, and the class was to be held the two days before Sara Jo's event.

I had initially come into contact with the prosthetic company Coyote Designs while researching alternative styles of sockets. I was always looking for the next best thing to improve my walking and had found that the direct approach always seemed to work out the best for me. The very feet I was walking on at that time were a type and style that I had wanted, but without insurance they were out of my reach. They were simply too cost prohibitive. Because Matt and Sienna had put me in front of so many different industry professionals, I had made a surprising list of contacts, and I began making calls and sending emails until I got the feet I wanted.

Sometimes the squeaky wheel gets the oil, and all of my polite pestering had paid off. Somehow a set of feet in my exact size had fallen off a truck right in front of Kentucky Prosthetics, and I had the advanced articulating ankle feet I wanted. They improved my walking immensely, and the experience taught me a valuable lesson. If you want something you need to go after it, and I applied that lesson to the new socket design. I called Coyote Designs to get some information, and was shocked when one of the owners of the company actually retuned my call. Coyote got together with Kentucky Prosthetics, and suddenly I was to be a test subject for their next course in Chicago. That was all well and good until I realized that I had to be in the Windy City on a Thursday and Friday, and then ride in a poker run back home on Saturday. It was what it was, and I couldn't change things, so I buckled down and dealt with a whirlwind few days.

The course and the university were both outstanding, and I was impressed with Northwestern. It is one of the leading schools in the country for prosthetics and orthotics, and it happened to be Sienna's alma mater. My own prosthetic glove design had been showcased at Northwestern several months earlier by a group of graduate students, and I was proud that the fingers I had made in my garage had made it into the halls of this storied institution.

I spent two days in Chicago with Coyote Designs and my own prosthetists Matt and Sienna, and when we were finally done, I spent a bit of time walking the streets of Chicago sightseeing with a friend who came into the city for the day to hang out. My friend Nicole was an amputee like myself, although her level of amputation is different from my own. She is a sports injury therapist as well as a college instructor, and we had met through the Amputee Coalition of America's social media outreach page.

I had no idea what to do in downtown Chicago so Nicole played the role of tour guide. I got to see some cool things down on the lakefront, have a really bad lunch with a really awesome person, and then fought with immigrant cab drivers trying to find a ride back to the airport for my flight home. With Nicole's help we finally convinced a cabbie born and bred in the south to make the rush-hour interstate ride out to the airport, and I was finally on my way home. A flight delay meant I would make it home at nearly midnight, and the very next morning I had to be out at the VFW post to prepare for Sara Jo's fundraiser.

There was food, raffle tickets, donated prizes, and the poker run setup to be dealt with, and I couldn't have done it on my own. In all honesty, the only thing I did was plan the event and make the necessary phone calls. The real credit for the entire thing goes to the good people at the Post. The Men's Auxiliary helped set up and then barbecue all the donated chicken and the members of the Ladies Auxiliary prepared all the rest of the food and then organized the plates and sales. The Post itself donated the use of the hall in the brand new building, so all I really needed to concern myself with was getting on my bike and riding in the poker run.

Our group of riders was chased the entire day by rain, but with a little bit of luck we never got wet. We had a diverse group of riders and all kinds of bikes, from the Harleys like Sara's mother Linda was riding, to the good looking old Suzuki that my friend William was on. The only bad spot in the day was when my own bike decided to break down, and less than fifteen miles from the end of the poker run I had to leave my bike on the side of the road and make the rest of the ride in a support vehicle.

Two of my friends and riding partners for the day, Tom Shockly and Lanny Allen, went back with a truck and picked up my bike for me, and it made it home before I did that night. The barbecue plates were sold and the raffle tickets were drawn, and we rounded out the night listening to a great local band called Cold Shot, who had donated their time for the event. All in all it was a great day, and we were able to raise some much needed funds to help Sara Jo toward her goal of walking again, but those three hard days of running took its toll on me. I had pushed myself beyond my limits, and I had to be practically carried out to the car for the ride home. Behcet's had reared its ugly head on my right knee, and I would spend the next two months nursing an ulcer on my kneecap.

A month after the benefit for Sara Jo, I received exciting news from Matt at Kentucky Prosthetics, it seemed that the prosthetics manufacturer Otto Bock had heard about my great progress, and wanted to feature me in an emergency services campaign along with two other amputee first responders. My knee had yet to heal, but I would not let that stop me from the opportunity to shine a spotlight on amputees in the emergency services.

The plan was for both a photo and video shoot with myself as a fire fighter, and two other patients from Kentucky Prosthetics; Joe Riffe, an above knee paramedic and fellow blogger, and Sgt. Kevin Trees, one of the few above knee amputees in the country serving as an active duty police officer. I had met both before, and I felt honored to be included in the project with both of these outstanding individuals. Joe had overcome overwhelming odds after a near fatal cliff fall to get back in an ambulance, and Kevin had made appearances on such programs as *The First 48* for his work as a homicide detective for the Louisville PD.

I might have had to use crutches during those few days of photo shoots and filming due to my knee, but I set them aside whenever I was in front of the camera. If I was going to be portrayed as contemporaries to the likes of Kevin and Joe, I preferred to do it on my own two feet. The entire thing was a great opportunity for me as I was allowed to beta test a new set of feet from Otto Bock, and they worked out well. The filming crew would eventually follow me home and shoot footage and interviews at the fire station, and I was very proud when both the publicity photos and the short films were released with Joe, Kevin, and me.

My knee eventually healed up and in the fall I returned to college to continue toward my goal of becoming a PTA. My knee healing also allowed me to finally get back to another sort of class. I was finally able to get back on the Jiu Jitsu mat. Earlier in the year I had begun a search for a trainer that would allow a triple amputee to train and study in their dojo. There are not many trainers that would consider taking on someone such as myself, first because of concerns of injury, and secondly because it would take a true forward thinker to devise a way to adapt all the moves meant for fully limbed individuals to someone who had considerably less.

I had two dojos that I wanted to get into, one that concentrated mainly on Jiu Jitsu, and another that offered the grappling arts as well as several more traditional arts. I had trained with both teachers in the past and I tried the grappling only school first, thinking that without other disciplines to get in the way the instructor could find the time to work through the challenges of training me. I was disheartened to find that I would be turned away; I had known the owners of the dojo for years, and yet they wouldn't let me on their mats for fear of my being hurt. As much as I tried I could not make them understand that even though I had lost my legs I was not fragile, but it did no good.

Having been rejected from one dojo, I did not hold high hopes for the other. The last time I had trained with this instructor the focus had been on both grappling arts and stand up arts such as Muay Thai boxing, incorporating the styles into a mixed martial arts program. In fact this dojo had trained and coached some MMA fight winners when I had trained there previously. I had always enjoyed the mat work much more, but had trained in the other MMA arts for the workout. The dojo had moved from its former location, and when I finally found the new location of Myers Martial Arts I was pleasantly surprised to find an entirely different sort of atmosphere in the dojo. Eric Myers still had the photos hanging on the wall from his earlier exploits as an MMA fight trainer, but as he explained it to me he decided he needed a change, and refocused his dojo toward more self-motivation, discipline, and self-defense. He now focused his concerns on helping his students better themselves through the arts, and he no longer had the urge to train ring fighters.

Eric accepted the thought of training a triple amputee as a true challenge, and although he could make me no promises, he would be more than glad to work with me. As simple as that, I was back on the mat and working out again. To my chagrin I found that my previous beltings in Nihon Ryu Jiu Jitsu, while still valid, could not be taken into consideration. Eric had been working for years up through the belt ranks of Gracie Brazilian Jiu Jitsu under Master Pedro Sauer, and he had finally achieved the rank of brown belt in that system - which allowed him to teach it.

I was getting back on the mat, but it would be as a white belt. I didn't really mind as I would have to learn everything again from my new legless perspective and starting over at white was just one more way of proving myself. My first time back on the mat was a bit awkward for everyone, as I was a bit of an oddity and no one really knew if I would still be able do any of the moves. Eric paired me up with a training partner and told me to try something basic that is familiar to every student of the art, an arm bar.

I couldn't really train with my prosthetics on, as carbon fiber and titanium could cause serious injury to anyone I worked with, so I started out crawling around on my hands and knees. It was definitely a different experience rolling without feet or calves, but muscle memory is muscle memory, and I easily worked my opponent into a side arm bar, cranked it down, and was quickly rewarded with a tap from my sparring partner.

That was all it took for Eric. "Yep, you're not going to have any problems. You're going to be able to do this."

I had only been back training a few short months when I blew up my knee at the fundraiser that July, and it would be October before I could begin training in earnest, but I had made it back on the mat and marked one more thing off my socket list.

The daily life I lead is not an easy one, before I can even get out of bed in the mornings I have to put on two prosthetic legs. Although the Behcet's disease doesn't haunt me nearly as often as it once did, I still have symptom flairs that can put me off my legs for weeks at a time. I live with the knowledge that I will be like this for the rest of my life, and know that I may one day grow too old or frail to continue using prosthetics. It will hopefully be a long time before I reach that point in my life, and every day until then I will strive to push myself to my limits, and then redefine those limits.

It has now been nearly three years since I lost my legs and I am not yet fully recovered from the atrophy, illness, and trauma. I have yet to cross some important things off my socket list, and I will most likely spend the rest of my life trying to define the two percent that I worry so much about. It has been a long road for me, and I am not done walking it yet. I am not yet finished with school, I have yet to fight a fire or make an ambulance run, and I still need to make it to the top of the training tower with harness and rope. I will get there. I will do those things. I will continue every single day to help those like me in any way I can, because that is all I ever really wanted to do. Help.

I survived coma and amputations. I learned to live again. I have begun walking. I will run. Every day I endeavor to climb, and I know that I will succeed. I have no doubts, and I will make no excuses. This is my life and I will not back down from it. I will never stop fighting.

I will always stand tough.

ACKNOWLEDGEMENTS

Writing my story has got to be one of the hardest things I have ever attempted to do in my life. So many people helped me in my road to recovery, and it will be hard to name them all, but I will try.

First and foremost, my family. Without the support of my parents, my brothers, my son, and my extended family I may not have ever even made it out of a bed and into a wheelchair. I love you guys very much! To every doctor, nurse, CNA, therapist, or health care worker that came into contact with me and helped me in the process, thank you. Doc Kitchens, you saved my life. Thank you sir, and keep rocking those Chuck Taylors.

Matt, Sienna, and everyone else at Kentucky Prosthetics... What can I say? You all are the best at what you do, and I wouldn't be where I am at now without your help and expertise!

During my recovery the Veterans of Foreign Wars Post 5484 was constantly pulling for me, and helped me out in so many ways. Both the Ladies' and Men's Auxiliaries played a huge part in fund raisers put on from me, and put on for me. John Wallace and Tom Shockly fired up a barbecue more than once for me and my friend's fund raisers, and I thank you for it. Tom recently passed away, and it breaks my heart that he wont get to read these words, but I will say them anyway - I knew Tom and I knew his father, and I feel I am a better human being for having done so. May they both rest in peace.

I couldn't talk about the Ladies' Auxiliary without mentioning those crazy cooking Turner sisters. Diane and Lisa literally made and served pounds and pounds of great food for us at events. Thank you and all the other Ladies that helped out. Tommy McCormick, Lanny Allen, and the rest of the Men's Auxiliary contributed in so many ways I am thankful for, and veteran Randy Nally never hesitated to donate the services of his hunting lodge to my cause. Thanks, guys, for all your efforts.

To all my friends of the RoC - Nick, Tilli, Knight, Deadly, Lola, Mofo, WEG!, and all the rest... Tea, Andrew, the crews at iSlaughter and Xenocide... You got me through some of my darkest times with your kind words and support.

Going back to college is tough, especially when you are on prosthetic legs, and all of my teachers need a big round of applause for putting up with me - especially Jennifer Welch. Thank you, Mrs. Welch, for putting up with my antics and my tardiness. When my son begins college I can only hope that he has instructors half as good as you.

To my editor Jenny Lee Smith, thank you for picking up the fumble. You were a life saver.

Last but not least I need to thank my Jiu Jitsu trainer Eric, and all my friends and rolling/sparring partners who have helped me along the way of my BJJ journey. Jiu Jitsu has done more for healing and strengthening my mind and body than anything else I have done since losing my legs. I hope to continue that journey for years to come with you all.

ABOUT THE AUTHOR

B Neil Brown is an author, writer and triple amputee who lives in Western Kentucky. He is an avid motorcycle rider, a retired Fire Fighter/EMT, and a Certified Entomologist. When not riding his bike or spending time with his son Neil can be found attending college working towards a degree in Physical Therapy, training in Gracie Jiu Jitsu, and designing/fabricating his own custom prosthetic digits.

Neil maintains a blog at www.twofeetshorter.com where he has documented his progress since becoming a bilateral trans-tibial and partial hand amputee. He frequently speaks to healthcare professional and student groups as well as amputee support groups, advocating for amputee care and sharing his story.

You can find him on Facebook at www.facebook.com/followtwofeetshorter or follow him on twitter @twofeetshorter

Made in the USA
Charleston, SC
10 June 2014